THINKING BIG

THINKING BIG

A history of Davis Langdon
Jim Meikle

black dog
publishing
london uk

Contents

Foreword

I have spent more than half my life with what is now Davis Langdon: 27 years as a partner and six of those as senior partner. I always knew that I was an inheritor of something significant, but I have been fascinated over the past couple of years by what has emerged during the research for this book on the firm's early days and its development.

Davis Langdon's origins stretch back to the early years of the last century and there is a clear progression to the firm today in its involvement with the best clients, the best designers and the best projects, and with its commitment to research and innovation. For a firm like Davis Langdon, growing as it has in recent years, it is instructive to be able to review where we have come from and how we got to where we are today. This history allows us to do just that.

There are very few written histories of firms like Davis Langdon and that is a pity; it would be good to compare and contrast. I hope that this effort will encourage others to collect and publish their stories. I also hope that this history will be of interest to our own people, past and current, but also to a wider readership.

My tenure as senior partner has been a roller coaster, with one of the most sustained booms and, possibly, the worst bust for 80 years. Publication of *Thinking Big* therefore comes at a very significant moment in the history of Davis Langdon.

The firm is now part of a global network and operates in an industry that is increasingly affected by global construction activity. There is therefore heightened expectation as to what consultants in our service area can provide by way of knowledge and experience. This is particularly relevant at a moment in time when clients in all sectors are looking ever more closely at their discretionary expenditure and are without exception calling for even faster and cheaper ways of doing things.

As I write this Foreword I still cannot see the bottom of the recession in the UK, and even those global markets that were performing well are now being adversely affected by the economic crisis. Nevertheless, I am confident that Davis Langdon knows where it stands and where it wants to get to. Its vision to push the limits with certainty is underpinned by its values. It understands that even greater innovation and collaboration with clients and colleagues will be required if we are to challenge boundaries. In addition, certainty will only come from advice and action delivered with integrity.

The firm's recent history has culminated in it being structured in a way in which it can directly engage with its clients. 90 years of history based around geography have been replaced with a sector focus. This change aligns Davis Langdon with the world in which it operates in that clients are seeking to work with ever more expert organisations with a real depth of capability.

The next part of the firm's history will record how *Thinking Big* will have influenced Davis Langdon's future success.

Rob Smith
senior partner, Davis Langdon LLP.

Thinking Big A History of Davis Langdon

Introduction

The purpose of compiling this history is to tell the story of the development of what has become Davis Langdon LLP, part of one of the largest firms of construction consultants in the world and to try to explain how and why it came to be that, from relatively modest beginnings. It may be of interest to members of the construction industry and others as an example of the successful growth and development of a major construction professional services firm. It should also be of interest to members of Davis Langdon, old and new.

The idea for this book has been around for some time and there have been a number of false starts. Some early members of the firm, though all too few, were forward looking enough to set down occasional notes and reminiscences. There are, for example, notes by Tom Every on the early days of Langdon & Every in the UK and the establishment of the firm in the Far East plus an account of the first 25 years of Davis Belfield & Everest written by Owen Davis, the founder of that part of the firm. There is also a series of *DB&E News* published in the 1960s and a single edition published in 1986; the weekly *Newsheet,* published since 1968; and *Grapevine,* an irregular in-house magazine produced from 1991. And there is the excellent Davis Langdon library.

Davis Langdon and the other firms that have helped create it over the past 80 odd years did not develop, grow and succeed in a vacuum. They are all creatures of their time and context. This book describes that context and relates the firms and their activities to it. It focuses on the people, offices and projects in Britain. It describes and discusses some of the firm's activities internationally, but these really deserve separate treatment.

The book begins with the merger of Langdon & Every and Davis Belfield & Everest in May 1988 because, in my view, that created the basis of today's firm. Without it, the individual firms would no doubt have flourished but, with it and with luck and good judgement, today's Davis Langdon is part of a major global enterprise. The merger was a big bold move and there have been more of these over the past 20 years.

Having described the merger, the book then goes back to tell the stories of the two firms from 1919 and 1931, respectively, up until 1988. They were involved in leading projects with the leading clients and designers of the day right from the start. They were also at the forefront of business and professional innovation. Four thematic chapters describe the establishment and growth of the firm nationally and internationally, the firm's diversification into a range of specialist services, and its activities in research and publishing. "Chapter Seven" covers the dozen or so years after the merger that transformed the firm into a modern business. The last chapter, "One Firm One Future", describes the firm today and reflects on its achievements and prospects.

Two of the problems with attempting to describe the early history are the lack of comprehensive written material on the firm and its people and projects, and the diversity of memories of surviving partners, members of staff and others. The first is something we have to accept, although more material may emerge in time. I have read through a mass of papers and documents from a wide range of sources and spoken to more than 100 people, partners, staff, clients, colleagues and others, in compiling this account. A debt of thanks is due to all my interviewees.

The diversity of memories is interesting. Apart from factual disagreements (the dates of specific events or the people and firms involved in particular projects), there were interesting variations in perceptions of the causes and effects of, for example, step changes in the firm's development. Some of this is, no doubt, unconscious (or even conscious) rewriting of history; some things are misremembered; and some are genuine differences of view. If readers could contribute their individual knowledge and information to correct errors and add to the story that would be very welcome. Work on the book has resulted in a greater interest in the history of Davis Langdon and the intention is to establish a company archive. Readers are encouraged to contribute their own recollections and related papers, photographs and other material.

Accounts of quantity surveying firms are rare. There are a few partial and unpublished histories of firms that I have seen, but the main published works are by James Nisbet and Gordon Aston. It would be good to think that this present publication will encourage other firms to at least record their corporate histories, if not publish the results. "Further Reading" lists the main publications that I have referred to.

Reflecting its colonial, not to say imperial, past, some of the terminology and place names used in the book are somewhat dated. The term Far East was used for many years to describe Langdon & Every's operations in Singapore, Hong Kong and elsewhere in what is now better known as South-East or East Asia. Arabian Gulf was the original suffix to what is now the Middle East practice. I have tended to use the terms appropriate to the context so they can vary. The firm's names also present problems; these are discussed in the "Explanatory Note on the Firm's Names" but, again, I have tried to use the names appropriate to the context.

Work on the book has been supported by Rob Smith, senior partner, and the Board of Davis Langdon LLP. It has been overseen by Rob and Jeremy Horner. A number of past and current partners and members of staff have also commented on the book as a work in progress. Finally, I have been ably assisted by Richard Parker, my research assistant, and encouraged by Duncan McCorquodale of Black Dog Publishing Limited, my publisher.

Chapter One

The Merger

In June 1986, two partners of two long established firms of chartered quantity surveyors, Ken Maclean of Langdon & Every (L&E) and Bill Fussell of Davis Belfield & Everest (DB&E), met for lunch at the East India Club.[1] During the meal, Maclean broached the idea of a merger of the two firms. Fussell was taken aback although his immediate inclination was to think it was an excellent idea. When they parted, Fussell went back to his partners at 5–7 Golden Square, on the edge of Soho, and reported the proposal.

These were the Thatcher years, the Conservative government having been re-elected in 1983. The miners' strike was over, the trade unions had been subdued; privatisation of the major state-owned enterprises was underway, British Gas was privatised in 1986; the deregulation of financial markets in October of the same year, precipitated radical changes in the City of London; and Nigel Lawson was Chancellor of the Exchequer and the so-called "Lawson Boom" was starting. It was a time of economic optimism and there was a feeling that the UK's reputation for industrial strife and poor economic performance was over.

The L&E partners had decided earlier in 1986 that their world was changing and that the future lay with the biggest or the very specialised and they needed to change too. They already had a wide international spread but a step change was needed. They wanted to increase the size and resources of the firm in order to service a perceived emerging class of global clients with construction projects around the world and who would welcome a construction cost adviser able to provide a consistent and high quality service in a range of locations. The answer was to identify another substantial firm and join forces.

The construction industry was changing rapidly and fundamentally, government was progressively withdrawing from leadership of the industry as sponsor and client (local authority housebuilding, for example, was now a few thousand a year, it had been 100,000 a year in the 1970s). A new generation of creative commercial developers was emerging, including Greycoat, Rosehaugh and Stanhope, all to become clients of the firm, and private commercial work was becoming the driver of construction demand.[2] The financial sector was internationalising in readiness for "Big Bang" in October 1986, and Canary Wharf had been identified as the flagship for both London Docklands and the property boom.

In 1983, mandatory fee scales were abandoned and it was now commonplace for quantity surveyors to compete on price for work, particularly for public sector work; and very few projects were now automatically allocated to selected firms. Prior to 1985, members of the Royal Institution of Chartered Surveyors (RICS) were not permitted to advertise, and firms were just beginning to adjust to the possibilities of marketing and public relations.

Top: Ken Maclean
Bottom: Bill Fussell

There were other permissible company structures, not just partnerships; it was possible, for example, for a firm of chartered surveyors to form Limited Liability companies or to be part owned by a commercial organisation. And contractors were permitted to take on professional roles, for example, on Design and Build and management forms of contracting.

The L&E partnership in the UK was seven strong in 1986. It comprised Maclean, Colin Brearley and Jim Driscoll, all about to retire, Alan Berryman, 60, Mike McLeod, in his early 50s and three younger partners. In 1984 they had had to adjust to the shock of Giles Every, their senior partner, dying in a car crash at the age of 54.

The L&E UK partners had a small but significant share in Langdon Every & Seah (LES) in South-East Asia, with offices in Singapore, Hong Kong, Indonesia, Malaysia, Brunei, The Philippines and Thailand and a joint venture business in Australia, and also owned Langdon and Every (Arabian Gulf) with offices in Bahrain, Doha, Abu Dhabi, Dubai and Sharjah. Overseas presences were common for UK professional services firms but L&E's in Asia was particularly long standing. The links between L&E and LES, however, were not that strong and needed attention. But at this stage, the merger was solely a UK initiative.

The L&E partners had identified their ideal criteria for a suitable merger partner. They wanted a firm that was in the top rank of UK quantity surveyors, did not overlap too much in terms of type of work and clients or geographically (at home and overseas), offered services and client relationships that would broaden their joint offering, and that they thought that they could work with. DB&E was at the top of the list.

DB&E was a successful but largely UK based practice (its Chester office had small offshoots in Bahrain and Kuwait). Its work was predominantly on buildings while L&E was also heavily involved in process and power engineering and the oil industry. Apart from London, there was only one city in the UK, Portsmouth, where both firms had offices. And DB&E's work and clients were firmly based in the UK. Despite their different backgrounds and operations, however, their key finances, including partners' drawings, were remarkably similar.

Maclean and Fussell, who had first discussed a possible merger, were both of a similar age and long-standing partners of their firms. Both were due to retire. Both had worked overseas in their early days: Maclean in the Middle East and Fussell in colonial Africa. They were sufficiently similar and sufficiently detached to be the right people to initiate things. They played little part in the subsequent discussions.

DB&E had more than 20 equity partners throughout the UK to L&E's seven but the initial approach was to the nine London partners who effectively owned and controlled DB&E. The non-London partners of DB&E only had an interest in their own offices. DB&E tended to move forward by consensus; they had only recently elected a senior partner, Geoff Trickey, having managed for their first five decades with a 'chairman of the partners'. L&E tended to be more autocratic and, having decided to initiate the merger process, tended to leave things to their senior partner, Maclean and then McLeod, who succeeded Maclean in August 1987. In 1987, L&E did not have any partner owners outside London.[3]

The proposition was debated long and hard within DB&E on the partners' floor of their Golden Square office. Most of the younger partners saw it as an opportunity to make a step change; Trickey, as senior partner, saw it as an opportunity to rethink and reorder the firm, and perceived these as worthwhile things to do, whether or not the merger went ahead. The views against a merger were mainly to do with innate conservatism and concerns about the partners entrusting their professional and financial success to people they didn't know. But, despite the reservations, it was agreed that discussions should continue. Initially, these were at least partly social occasions where the partners could meet and get to know each other; subsequently they became more serious and more focused.

External financial and legal advisers were recruited and the partners themselves were each delegated, mostly in pairs, one from each firm, to examine different aspects of the business, including for example structure, organisation, finances, marketing and IT. There were regular meetings in the Institute of Directors (IoD) in Pall Mall with rooms booked under a password and with both sets of partners entering and leaving the building separately. The process was long and thorough, and yielded much interesting information for all parties but did not come up with any insuperable barriers. Heads of Agreement were signed in late summer 1987. A key element was that the merged firm would be a partnership, not a company.

All the L&E UK partners were involved in the original decision to seek a merger partner and the subsequent negotiations. The DB&E London partners now felt able to approach their provincial partners. Although some of them had an inkling that 'something' was going on, generally it came as a surprise when they were told that a merger, particularly one like this, was on the cards. Again, most of them were enthusiastic, some because 'bigger was better'; some because the idea of restructuring the firm was attractive and, potentially, to their personal advantage; some because the international links were attractive; and some because broadening the range of services and project types matched their own aspirations. To some extent, the London partners were less diverse in both their geographical spread and their range of activities; they had less need to be. Arguably the non-London partners had to work harder and look further afield for their workload and income.

The L&E partners did not have UK branch partners to consult, but they did have the partners of LES in South-East Asia to consider. The main link between L&E in the UK and LES, apart from the UK firm's profit share, was attendance by the UK senior partner at the Far East partners' conference in October of each year. McLeod of L&E and Nick Davis of DB&E (the latter standing in for Trickey, who was unwell) attended the October 1987 conference in Bangkok and presented the idea of the UK merger to the Far East partners. They were intrigued; the merger had long-term potential and had no financial downside for them. There were no objections.

By early 1988, the details of the merger were more or less agreed and, within the partnerships, those that had to be had been informed. The next hurdle was to manage the announcement to the staff of both firms, the industry and the press. One of the most remarkable aspects of the whole thing was that, up until the public announcement in March 1988, the blanket of secrecy was virtually complete. There are stories of telephone technicians coming into Golden Square and announcing , but only to the receptionists, that they had to link up the telephone lines with Aldwych House (L&E's London office). The exchange was overheard by Cliff Lawson, the DB&E office manager and privy to the merger. Lawson quickly silenced the technicians and swore the receptionists to secrecy.

Inevitably, however, rumours began to circulate that something was brewing. In a pre-emptive move the DB&E partners circulated a memo, prior to the staff announcement of the merger, stating that they should make every effort to attend a meeting to hear the firm's plans for its future organisation and referring to "the revised structure that this would necessarily entail". This left many to conclude, wrongly of course, that the firm was about to list on the Alternative Investment Market. Yorke Rosenberg Mardall (YRM), a major firm of architects and well known to DB&E, had just done this and it had received wide coverage in the technical press. The idea that DB&E was considering a listing was plausible. And, although it risked being perceived as the partners 'cashing in', it had the major plus of diverting observers from the real change.

In the period from January to March 1988, an enormous amount of effort was put into when, where and how the news of the merger was to be announced to the staff of the two firms and how the merged firm was to

be presented to the wider world. Furneaux Stewart, a firm of communications and design consultants, working with two of the partners (Paul Morrell of DB&E and Derek Lawrence of L&E), devised a new corporate image and launch strategy. Lawrie Stewart of Furneaux Stewart had, in fact, been working with DB&E prior to the merger discussions to develop a new house style for the firm and this went on in parallel, switching focus to the merger and the new branding in Autumn 1987.

Four new partners were appointed by DB&E at the time of the merger: Richard Baldwin and Neill Morrison in London, Paul Edwards, in South Wales, and Jim Meikle, in the Consultancy Group based in London.

Photographs had to be taken for a launch video and photographers going round Golden Square and Aldwych House prompted curiosity from those not in the know.

The announcement to the staff was made at a joint presentation at the IoD in March 1988. There are a number of amusing, and mostly true, stories of DB&E staff being met by DB&E partners on their way out of the IoD. Having been told they should go back in they said "I'm in the wrong place. It's full of L&E people." And the same applied to L&E staff.

The launch video was played and statements were made by Geoff Trickey and Mike McLeod, their first public roles as joint senior partners of Davis Langdon & Everest, the name of the merged firm. The IoD audience was simultaneously surprised and impressed. Owen Davis, the founder of DB&E, was in the audience and was reported to be unhappy at the idea of the merger, remarking that his "corner shop was becoming a supermarket". At the time, DB&E was one of the largest and most successful quantity surveying firms in the country; his corner shop analogy seemed a bit extreme. Davis accepted the merger, like other changes, and never sought to interfere. Clearly the firm had changed since his days (he had retired in 1973) and the merger would take it further from the traditional partnership he had known.

The announcement was accompanied by an eight page leaflet highlighting the work and resources of the new firm and its aspirations. The leaflet put down markers for a range of new service offerings, including project management, management consultancy and legal support services. It also introduced the globe and star logo, originally L&E mustard yellow and DB&E blue, representing the world and the firm's plans to be a major player.

Inevitably, the new name was the focus of much attention but in the end, knowing that initials would be adopted for general use, everyone was

Geoff Trickey, left, and Mike McLeod, right.

DAVIS BELFIELD & EVEREST
LANGDON AND EVERY

ANNOUNCEMENT

From the first of May 1988,
DAVIS BELFIELD & EVEREST and
LANGDON & EVERY will merge
to form the largest practice of
Quantity Surveyors in the world.
The new firm will be called
DAVIS LANGDON & EVEREST.
It will be able to offer clients the
resources of over 1100 staff, operating from 18 offices throughout
the United Kingdom and another
15 offices in 15 countries around
the world.

DAVIS LANGDON & EVEREST
CHARTERED QUANTITY SURVEYORS

persuaded that DL&E, which combined two initials from each of the firms
was the most acceptable. McLeod and Trickey agreed at the outset to leave
the decision on the name to the last moment arguing that, if by then every
other matter had been agreed, no one would want an argument over
the name to jeopardise the merger.

The press was informed in a separate press briefing at the Café Royal, also by
Trickey and McLeod. The technical press was generally favourably impressed
by the merger and *Building* magazine awarded it the privilege of their front

The cover of the merger leaflet with
the firm's new identity and name at
bottom right.

cover on 1 April 1988: a rather odd photograph of the new joint senior partners and the headline "Surveying the World". The leading article began "The earth seldom moves for quantity surveyors. But yesterday it did." The national press picked up the firm's press release and gave the merger some coverage but they were relatively disinterested by a merger of, to them, two small unlisted private firms.

At the same time as the announcement at the IoD, all the provincial offices of DB&E and L&E showed the video and circulated the leaflet. If anything, the enthusiasm in the non-London offices was greater than even that of the London people. They were excited at the opportunities of new services and new areas of operation.

The construction industry was also impressed. It was perceived by most firms and individuals in the industry as a bold strategic move that would almost certainly lead to a step-change in the prospects of the merged firm. There were lots of other corporate changes, associations and other things going on but this was perceived as both unusual and impressive. The quantity surveyors, in particular, were impressed, it was seen as forward-looking, it made sense, it was big news at a time when marketing had become respectable.

Having announced the merger to staff and the world at large, the next thing was to make it work. Although the partners by this time knew each other reasonably well, the challenge was to get the staff talking and working with each other. The first and main problem was contact and communication. The two London offices were a mile apart, everyone was incredibly busy and there were few immediate opportunities for doing things together. And, apart from Portsmouth, outside London, the firms' offices were in different cities.

Immediately after the launch, the search was on for a new London office that would accommodate the staff of the merged firm and anticipated expansion. Market conditions were good for landlords, there was strong demand for office space, rents were high and availability was low. Furthermore, attractive offices in the right location were essential to retain staff. A survey of staff was undertaken to establish how they travelled to work, where from and where they would like to work. The majority lived more than an hour's commute from either Golden Square or the Aldwych; nobody wanted a longer, more complicated or more expensive journey to work; and everyone wanted to be in central London with easy access to mainline railway stations.

The partners decided that they wanted around 35,000 square feet, rather more than the combined Golden Square (approximately 20,000 square feet) and Aldwych House (approximately 9,000 square feet) premises, to accommodate 350 people, rather more than the combined headcount. And they wanted their own front door in a good building in a good location. This was relatively scarce in the London commercial property market, particularly in boom conditions. It took more than a year but eventually Princes House in Kingsway was identified as suitable and plans were made to refurbish, furnish and equip it to an appropiate standard. The office environment was to be another step-change.

Duffy Eley Giffone & Worthington (DEGW), architects and space-planners, were commissioned to produce layouts for Princes House and to select the furniture. The building was in two wings and on eight floors and was, with hindsight and the subsequent experience of MidCity Place, not the most effective or efficient office space. It was, however, an improvement on the previous accommodation of both firms and the staff in general liked it. Princes House was also installed with a suite of fully furnished meeting rooms and a board room *cum* dining room on the top floor with an impressive view over Covent Garden and the West End.

The former L&E people moved into Princes House in January 1990; the DB&E people followed from Golden Square in July 1990, just as the Lawson commercial property boom was beginning to deflate. There were three years remaining on the Aldwych House 30 year lease and the landlord was happy to buy that back as they were in the midst of refurbishing the whole building. The DB&E 20 year lease, tidily, was coming to an end and, shortly after they left, the Golden Square building was demolished and rebuilt.

A new management structure was introduced immediately after the merger. It was, inevitably, rather more formal than either firm was used to. Overall management of the UK firm was vested in a management board of nine partners, headed by the joint senior partners, and representing both London and non-London offices. Under the board there were eight committees, Partnership, Finance, Professional, Marketing, New Services, New Locations, Administration and Staff, and under the Professional and Staff committees there were a further nine sub-committees. The principal advantage of that number of committees and sub-committees was that it involved most partners and associates and other senior staff and helped let them get to know each other; the obvious disadvantage was that it was time consuming and inefficient. Perhaps because the organisation and management of the two firms before the merger was relatively simple, there was very little duplication of roles and, hence, few redundancies.

McLeod and Trickey were not only joint senior partners but also retained project responsibilities as team partners. The new firm adopted the DB&E

organisational structure whereby the London office was divided into teams headed by two or three equity partners and each with their own hierarchy of associates and senior surveyors. Teams tended to focus on particular clients, designers or types of work. The assumption was that running the firm was at most a part-time job.

The ownership model adopted was also DB&E's, a kind of franchise with the London partners holding a share in all the branch offices and the branch partners only having an interest in their own office. After the merger, there was a total of 35 equity partners, 15 in London and the remainder in 18 offices around the country. The total included six new partners, two in London and four in branch offices. A 'national account', funded by a levy of 20 per cent of profit on all offices was partly used to pay for whole firm expenses, e.g. advertising and promotion, and partly recycled to offices in proportion to their share in the business. The firm's financing was based on working capital provided by the partners and annual drawings were based on that year's results.

Reorganisation of the management, ownership and finances of the firm was to become a major theme of partners discussions over the following years but the agreement arrived at in 1988 allowed the firm to move forward immediately as a going concern. It attempted, more or less successfully, to combine the hands-on control of a traditional partnership with more formal management arrangements. It did not, however, satisfactorily resolve the participation of the branch partners in the new business.

Staff terms and conditions and, in particular, the pension scheme had to be standardised. The aim was always to make people no worse off and generally, therefore, the result was a levelling upwards in terms or conditions or monetary compensation where things were changed or terminated. Since the industry was booming, there was a general shortage of qualified people and attracting and retaining staff was a priority. A major attraction in those less-environmentally sensitive times was a car for all qualified people. The other staff innovation was appointment of a dedicated Human Resources person, a relatively rare appointment at the time for a professional firm. There was an increasing consciousness of the importance of staff relations, partly to ensure that the best people were retained and partly to handle an increasingly complex legal and administrative framework.

Amidst all the reorganisation, there was, of course, a business to run, and one with a full order book. At the end of their first year the new firm was over 600 strong and had a total fee income of £21.5 million. Its business was primarily quantity surveying, or cost management, and its services fairly traditional. It had to serve its clients as well as reshape itself. Major ongoing projects at the time of the merger included The British Library in London, designed by Colin St John Wilson, Sizewell B Power Station on the Suffolk coast, the Waterloo International Terminal, designed by Nicholas Grimshaw, John Lewis at Kingston, designed by Ahrends Burton & Koralek, and Stockley Park, with buildings designed by Norman Foster and others.

Diversification was flagged up in the merger brochure as a future strategy. It was partly in response to client demand, partly because individuals in the firm wanted to do other things and partly a reaction to the introduction of fee competition. Distinct services could be charged for, not just included in the quantity surveying fee. It was also recognition that the merged firm was not just bigger but also different. With the merger, Consultancy had become a separate profit centre, although it had been in existence for five years or so; a Project Management group was established in London under Derek Johnson, who became a partner two years later; and there were the beginnings of Legal Support Services and Construction Taxation. But the reality was that the vast majority of the firm's fee income was from traditional quantity surveying services and these were still very traditional in nature.

The merger, of course, was only of the two UK firms. There was much to be done on the international front. A major part of the *raison d'être* for the merger was the potential international market and the firm's presence in the Middle East and in Asia. It would have been impossible to try to bring together the international practices at the same time as the UK merger but international consolidation was always the aim and the UK partners now turned their attention to the links with L&E (Arabian Gulf) and LES.

A single legal entity would have been difficult to engineer, particularly reconciling ownership, different corporate structures and different tax regimes but there was great scope for closer links that would create an organisation offering common standards of service around the world. The aim was for a global umbrella under which the existing firms could operate and to which others could be introduced as opportunity and circumstances permitted.

One key problem was how to link the firms on a basis that was not only equal but in fact looked equal. L&E (AG) had local partners but was majority owned by the UK partners, so any decision about their incorporation was largely a matter for the UK. LES was a large successful practice in its own right and would not accept any arrangement that looked as though they were an offshoot of the UK. After much debate amongst a small group of

UK partners the idea of an umbrella organisation, Davis Langdon & Seah International (DLSI), linked to a name-change to Davis Langdon & Seah in Asia, emerged. This gave equal recognition to all with an emphasis on the essential 'Seah' element in South-East Asia and it was the equivalent of the combination of the original firms' names in the UK.

Mike McLeod had suggested previously to LES that they might change their name to DLS to strengthen the global image but had been rebuffed by the LES partners who saw it as a 'Davis Langdon'-dominated name and were concerned that in any new ventures it would be the 'S' (Seah) that would be dropped. The UK partners now saw the addition of 'International' linked to Davis Langdon and Seah, as the international firm's name, as the solution, but they still had to sell it to sceptical partners in Asia. A group of around ten UK partners drawn from London and other offices attended the LES conference in Hong Kong in 1989 to strengthen the links, get to know each other better and try to reach agreement on the international firm. The turning point was Paul Morrell's presentation to the LES partners on the issue of the firm's name; the LES partners liked it. It embedded the Seah name in the firm's title, and they accepted the proposal. This was a major step forward.

Having settled upon a name, the remainder of the international discussions went relatively smoothly. Basically the financial relationship remained the same with the UK partnership retaining an interest in the Far East practice and the Middle East practice becoming ever closer to the UK. The largest firm of quantity surveyors in the world had been created.

The international association led to a redesign of the firm's stationary. A dark red "Davis Langdon & Seah International" striped bar was introduced at the bottom of letterheads and other documents; the names of partners were removed (the list, in any case, was becoming too long); the L&E yellow in the logo was changed to the same dark red.

Top: John Lewis, Kingston, Ahrends Burton & Koralek.

Centre left: Sizewell B Power Station, from Berry Ritchie, *The Good Builder: The John Laing Story*, p. 173.

Centre right: The British Library, Colin St John Wilson.

Bottom: Waterloo International Terminal, Nicholas Grimshaw & Partners.

Photographer: Roman von Gotz/Bildarchiv Monheim/arcaid.co.uk.

In 1989, there was already evidence of over-supply of commercial property, a key driver of construction demand and, in late 1990, Chancellor Lawson raised bank base rates to 15 per cent and the property boom was effectively over. New orders peaked in 1991 and did not recover these levels until 1998.

It is difficult to date precisely when the market turns and it turns at different times for different people. Architects tend to be the first to feel a drop in demand; quantity surveyors may not feel it for some months or even a year. It was 1991 before DLE responded by reducing staff numbers and it was the financial year 1991/1992 before there was a drop in income. In fact, DL&E

was probably better placed than some of its competitors to ride the coming recession. It had large long-term contracts, its main clientele was public sector, and work was still coming in, just not as much as it had become used to. It was still a painful period for partners and staff.

Commentary

From the perspective of 20 years on, the merger still looks like absolutely the right thing to have done. Davis Langdon has an unrivalled name and reputation and is still the largest firm of quantity surveyors in the world. It is an admired and respected firm involved in most of the major projects of the day and offers a wider range of construction related professional services than even the merger leaflet anticipated. Without the merger, DB&E and L&E would probably still have been in the top rank but not necessarily at the top.

L&E had been founded just after the First World War and was an established firm with long-term blue chip clients, including BP, Ascot, the Jockey Club, the Bank of England and the Central Electricity Generating Board (CEGB) and the largest network of associated overseas firms of any UK firm. DB&E was founded in the early 1930s and had an impressive record in mainly public buildings and a reputation in publication and research. Both firms were well into the second and third generations of partners; both also recognised that their world was changing and that would require them to change.

Mergers are as much about style as content and, in retrospect, it has been the DB&E style or 'culture' that has tended to prevail, at least in the UK, and it has been DB&E people that have led the firm. After the joint tenure of McLeod and Trickey, the subsequent senior partners, Nick Davis, Paul Morrell and Rob Smith, have all come from the DB&E side of the firm. The L&E element that has prevailed is, of course, the overseas one, and it has expanded. Davis Langdon & Seah in Asia remains a major player in its market and it has grown in numbers and locations. Davis Langdon LLP has substantially reshaped its UK and Middle East business and, through DLSI, it has also grown and developed in Africa, Australasia, New Zealand and North America.

Interestingly, the "One Firm One Future" initiative, introduced in 2008 is more akin to L&E's single national firm model than DB&E's centre and branches model. It is intended to focus on sector and service specialisms and to do away with competition between teams and offices. A strapline on the 1988 merger leaflet "One Firm, One Aim, One Future" was a portent. It has just taken 20 years to get there.

In retrospect, the timing of the merger was nearly perfect. It was concluded just before the peak of the market, when the main players were confident and financially secure. Two or three years later, as the industry slid into recession, there may not have been the stomach for such a bold move.

Tom Every did not live to see the merger, he died in February 1987. Owen Davis and Ken Maclean both attended the merger announcement event at the Institute of Directors. Maclean, as an initiator of the merger was clearly enthusiastic; Davis graciously said to Maclean that he was not keen but, if it had to be any firm, he was pleased that it was L&E. On reflection, Davis' concerns were partly because he was a traditionalist but also because he saw the merger as a 'business' decision, while to him, partnership decisions were about individuals.

In 2009 there are only two equity partners who were partners before the merger, Rob Smith, now senior partner and Simon Johnson, now Managing Partner of Davis Langdon, Europe and the Middle East, plus two who became partners at the time of the merger, Neill Morrison, and Richard Baldwin. Many people now in the firm are only vaguely aware that there was a merger in 1988 and, in any case, there have been a number since. But without the vision and actions of a dozen or so individuals 20 years ago, there would not be the Davis Langdon there is today.

1   Abbreviations of the firms' names will be used throughout. This creates problems of clarity and consistency and an explanatory note is provided at the end of the book to help readers negotiate these.

2   Private commercial output represented nine per cent of total demand in 1980 and over 20 per cent at the end of the decade; public housing fell from seven per cent to two per cent over the same period. New office building accounted for about one third of all new commercial building work nationally and two thirds in the South-East.

3   Jim Driscoll, based in Southampton, retired in 1986.

Chapter Two

Early Years

Langdon & Every (L&E) and Davis Belfield & Everest (DB&E) were both established in the years between the First and Second World Wars. L&E was founded by Horace Langdon in 1919, a year after the First World War ended and DB&E was founded 12 years later by Owen Davis. Langdon started in practice at 6 Raymond Buildings, Gray's Inn, and Davis at 34 Red Lion Square, both close to the firm's current London office on High Holborn. Langdon was 40 years old when he started in practice, had been surveyor to the War Department during the First World War but only qualified in 1920; Davis was 23 and newly qualified when he started practice in 1931.

The First World War formally ended with the signing of the Armistice on 11 November 1918. The new era was quickly very different in almost every way from the Edwardian world before the war. Universal male suffrage came that year and, at the same time, women over the age of 30 were given the vote. Economic growth between the wars averaged just under three per cent but the growth was erratic and the structure of the economy was changing. The traditional heavy industry was in decline and the growth industries were artificial fibres, electrical machinery and motor vehicles. Electricity was replacing steam power and transport was increasingly powered by petrol engines. Unemployment was never less than ten per cent over the period and it was over 20 per cent in 1931 and 1932. The period also included the General Strike in 1925 and the Wall Street Crash in 1929.

The political situation was complex. There were concerns about Bolshevism in Russia and the rise of Fascism in Germany and Italy and, at home, Ireland was a continual source of concern. The new Labour Party emerged in 1918 and rapidly attracted support; the first Labour government came to power in 1924. The domination of the domestic political scene by the Conservative and Liberal Parties was over.

Construction had started changing in terms of industrial organisation, materials and technology before the First World War but the period between the First and Second World Wars was to see increasing rates of change. Masonry and timber were being replaced by brick, concrete and steel; loadbearing by framed structures; and Gothic, Classical and Arts and Crafts styles were giving way to Art Deco and International Modern. But, for much of the period, all of these technologies and styles were evident.

Before the First World War, the government's role in construction was relatively insignificant, but from 1919 government policy had a considerable influence on the industry. Subsidies were provided to encourage housebuilding and local authorities built public housing on a scale never seen before. Over 40 per cent of houses built between the wars were subsidised and nearly one third were built by local authorities.

Construction, particularly housebuilding, was a major employer in the 1920s and 1930s, particularly the latter years of the 1930s (after the depression that dominated the early part of the decade). Non-residential building was also significant, with major redevelopment in the City of London and a range of other buildings, including factories, cinemas and public buildings.

Most surprisingly, from today's perspective, general prices and construction prices fell for most of the period. In 1938 the average cost of construction was roughly two thirds what it had been in 1920. The fall was erratic, most dramatically between 1921 and 1922 with a slight recovery in 1925 and in the late 1930s.

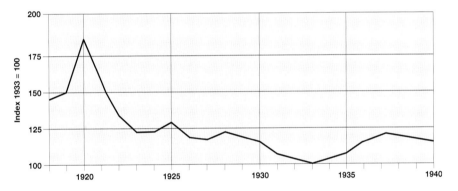

Quantity surveying was an established occupation in 1919, a number of firms had been in existence for decades.[1] Its origins probably date back to the seventeenth century and the Great Fire of London, when they were called "measurers". In the middle of the nineteenth century, however, as a reaction to large overspends on some public projects, procedures were developed so that contractors gave bids for buildings before work commenced. Up to that time they undertook work as it was required and were paid at the end on a time and materials basis. This new process brought about the need for contractors to not only have drawn information but also a clear description of what was required in terms of the quantity of work. Contractors quickly realised that it did not make much sense for all tenderers on a job to produce their own quantities so they got together and appointed one person or firm to undertake the measurement: the quantity surveyor. The list of measurements was called a bill of quantities.

Graph showing retail price inflation between the wars. Source: Office for National Statistics (ONS).

The key distinction between the old measurers and the new quantity surveyors was that the former measured the work after it was undertaken;

the latter, before. Early in the twentieth century, architects began to send out bills of quantities with the drawings and specification, thus architects were responsible for recommending, if not appointing, the quantity surveyor. Quantity surveyors were often paid by a percentage addition to their bills of quantities. Their main roles were to compile the bills, prepare interim valuations and settle final accounts.

In 1919, The Surveyors' Institution, forerunner of the Royal Institution of Chartered Surveyors (RICS), was 50 years old and had around 500 quantity surveying members out of a total membership of less than 5,000. The quantity surveyors were intent on establishing themselves as a distinct profession: the Quantity Surveyors Committee was formed in 1904, the first scale of fees was prepared in 1913 and the first Standard Method of Measurement was published in 1922.[2] In the 1920s, however, quantity surveying was still a fairly obscure occupation.

Langdon & Every

William Horace Langdon, a first son, was born in 1879, and spent his youth in Callington, ten miles North-West of Plymouth, at the eastern edge of Cornwall. His father died in his 30s in the late 1880s and William, as he was then known, was brought up by his mother, with four younger brothers, in relatively modest circumstances. In the early years of the twentieth century as a young man, he was lodging in Ilford in Essex and the 1901 census records him as a draughtsman. He apparently met his wife to be, Fanny Amelia, in Ilford and they were married in Romford in 1904. Fanny's father was a brick manufacturer. Interestingly, on the marriage certificate, William Horace appears as Horace William, a style he retained for the rest of his life.

The details of Langdon's career prior to the First World War are hazy. He is recorded as studying part time at the City of London College, an institution dedicated to the professional education of working men but it is not known what he studied. Tom Every thought that Langdon had worked as an estimator for the contractors Holloways, before the War.[3] The 1911 census has him living in west London with his wife and one year old daughter and his occupation as assistant manager with a builder and decorator.

Langdon's obituary in the *RICS Journal* notes that he "had wide experience in a number of private and public offices in Callington, Cornwall, in Devon, Southend and London". We know nothing about his working in Callington, his birthplace, Devon or Southend. It is interesting to speculate how he progressed from a draughtsman to an assistant manager with a building contractor to an important public post in just over ten years. According to his *RICS* obituary, he was appointed as surveyor to the War Department after being five times refused for service with the armed forces. His work during the war seems to have been the launchpad for his future success.

Langdon started in practice in 1919. He was 40 and not yet a qualified quantity surveyor; he qualified as a Professional Associate of the Surveyors' Institution (PASI) in 1920. His first office was at 6 Raymond's Buildings in Gray's Inn but he moved a year later to 57/58 Chancery Lane, a building now occupied by the London Silver Vaults. One of his neighbours, across the road was Northcroft Neighbour & Nicholson, a rather more established firm. The practice was to stay in Chancery Lane until 1928 when it moved to 292 High Holborn, almost directly opposite Davis Langdon's present office in MidCity Place.

It was a difficult time to start a firm; work was hard to come by and Langdon apparently augmented his income by coaching students for examinations and writing on building and architectural matters. He also took on a number of loss assessments in Ireland for landowners whose property had been damaged or destroyed in the early 1920s. The British government had guaranteed the landowners protection and set up a commission to examine claims. It was difficult, although not impossible, for this kind of work to be done by Irish surveyors and Langdon seems to have impressed both the commission and the landowners.[4]

Tom Every, like Langdon, from a West Country family, was born in 1902. He came from a relatively well-off family of Devon brewers and had gone to school at University College School in North London. He completed his articles as a general practice surveyor with Weatherall & Green in Chancery Lane but during his studies with Parr Adkin & Blake (forerunner of the College of Estate Management) he met Cyril Sweett, then with Gardiner & Theobald, and others and was introduced to quantity surveying. At that time finding a job was difficult, but through an old school friend he was introduced to Langdon and joined him in October 1922. He was not the first recruit; the staff at the time included John Belmont Taylor, a pupil of Langdon's.

In 1924, Every was appointed resident quantity surveyor on Stewart & Arden's Morris motor car showroom, workshop and distribution centre in Acton. The architect was Arthur Davis, another old boy of University College School, and he had asked to have Every on site. Morris was an important enterprise and Stewart and Arden were sole agents in London and the Home Counties. Every spent 18 months on this project and, on his return to Chancery Lane, he and Taylor were offered partnerships.

Tom Every recalls Taylor as "a brilliant quantity surveyor but as soon as he became a partner he spent all his time to begin with checking and amending the draft partnership deed which had not yet been signed". This was a bad omen and soon afterwards Langdon and Every resolved to get rid of Taylor which Every notes "took a long time and a great deal of money to do so". The partnership was dissolved in 1928 and a notice to that effect appeared in *The Times*. Taylor then not only left the firm but a couple of years later disappeared from the records of the Surveyors Institution.

In parallel with establishing his firm, Horace Langdon worked hard at achieving status and reputation in the local community in Holborn, in the surveying profession and in the Masons. He was a member of Holborn Borough Council from 1925 and was mayor of Holborn in 1936. As a result, he had a council residential block named after him in the 1960s, Langdon Buildings in Leather Lane.

Langdon was chairman of the City and Guilds of London Institute Advisory Committee on Quantity Surveying (QS) from 1922; chairman of the QS division of the Surveyors' Institution from 1933 to 1935; chairman of the QS section of the International Congress of Surveyors in 1934; and he was chairman of the North-West London branch of the Institution in 1935. He was also a member of three Masonic lodges and Worshipful Master of the Holborn Borough Council Lodge in 1935 and active in a number of overseas lodges. And he was a great golfer; in the mid-1930s he claimed to have played on nearly 500 European courses; at the time of his death his obituary suggested 600.

Tom Every, though much younger, was encouraged by his senior partner to participate in public affairs. He was elected as a Guardian of the Poor for the Chair of Holborn & Finsbury in 1925 but these positions were abolished shortly afterwards. Every remarked later that it was valuable experience but that it "cured me of having any desire for any sort of political life". Apparently, he did not join the Masons. He was, however, involved with the Surveyors Institution but not greatly, initially, as the firm could not afford two partners being heavily engaged in institutional matters.

The firm worked on a range of projects, usually as a result of good relations with architects. In the 1920s they worked with Riley & Glanfield on projects for the London County Council (forerunner of the Greater London Authority), including the North-Western Polytechnic in Kentish Town (subsequently subsumed in what has become the University of North London) and the conversion of Old County Hall in Spring Gardens next to Admiralty Arch, when the new County Hall was completed on the South Bank. They also worked together on the addition of a floor to the Kodak Building (Nos.

61–63) in Kingsway. Riley & Glanfield were also established in 1919 in Gray's Inn, so they may well have been neighbours of Langdon's. At around the same time, Langdon worked with a firm called Harrington & Evans on projects in Romford in Essex, including a cinema, the greyhound racing track and a new isolation hospital.[5]

From the late 1920s the firm worked with Seely & Paget on a number of projects, many of them country houses, including the extension and adaptation of Eltham Palace for the Courtauld family and extensions to Laverstoke in Hampshire for Sir Wyndham Portal. John Seely, later Lord Mottistone, and Paul Paget met at Cambridge and started in practice in the early 1920s. Both were from prominent families and, in addition to work on country houses, were specialists in the restoration of historic churches. The relationship with Seely & Paget continued until well after the Second World War.

Langdon and Every also worked with George Grey Wornum, architect of the RIBA building, before and after the war. And they worked with Brian Sutcliffe, formerly with Riley & Glanville, on alterations to Moulton Paddocks in Newmarket, a mansion owned by Dudley Joel, businessman and politician. This may have been the firm's introduction to the world of horse racing that was to be a significant part of their business after the war.

The early 1930s were difficult years for the firm and the industry in general. In an attempt to generate new and different sources of work, Langdon made contact with the Bingley Building Society (now Bradford & Bingley) who were

Opposite top: Notice of 'partnerships dissolved' in *The Times*, 11 January 1928.
Copyright *The Times*.
Opposite centre: Tom Every.
Opposite bottom: Horace Langdon in his mayoral robes, 1936.
Above: The entrance to Eltham Palace remodelled for the Courtauld family by Seely & Paget.

thinking of expanding outside of Yorkshire.[6] The firm assisted them in this and the society opened an office in Kingsway with Aubrey Lawrence as their manager in London. HWL&E were duly appointed as surveyors for all their work in the South of England and this helped tide the firm over a difficult period. With the outbreak of war all new housing stopped and the building society shrank to a skeleton staff and closed their London office. Lawrence was taken on by HWL&E in an administrative role and shortly after became company secretary.

In 1932, Eric Watson, who had been with the firm for ten years or so, decided to go out to the colonies and work for a building contractor in Singapore. Five years or so later, Frank Angell, a contemporary of Watson also left for Singapore. These two briefly went into private practice before the Japanese invasion.

Unusually for the time, HWL&E established branch offices in the 1930s, in Southampton and Stoke on Trent. They were opened respectively by John Winship and Edward Thornton-Firkin both from the London office. After a short time these two were both offered local partnerships and new firms of Langdon Every & Winship and Langdon Every & Firkin were founded. Their stories are told in "Chapter Five".

Before the war, Every had joined the Officers' Emergency Corps and was called up to join the Royal Engineers but was sent back because quantity surveying was a reserved occupation. In January 1941 he was called into the Ministry of Works to take charge of air raid damage in the three regions of the South-East of England, excluding London, Reading, Cambridge and Tunbridge Wells. His counterpart in the London region was an architect, JM Wilson, who a few years later was to introduce him to the Anglo Iranian Oil Company. Latterly, Every was appointed as Director of Post War Building Programmes, directly under Lord Portal, Minister of Works, HWL&E's old client. He was involved in a range of planning activities, including working on the Simon Committee report on the construction industry, and was awarded a CBE in the 1946 New Year's Honours List in recognition of his services.

On the night of 8/9 September 1940, the first air raid on London in the Second World War, the firm was bombed out of the office in High Holborn. They had only a relatively small staff as most people were on sites across the country but the firm's records were destroyed. For four months they shared offices with architect Brian Sutcliffe in Manchester Square and then moved to a suite of offices on the top floor of 20/23 Lincoln's Inn Fields. This building was requisitioned as the headquarters of the Canadian Air Force in 1942 and the firm moved again to Kingsway House, 103 Kingsway, on the first floor.

Throughout the war the firm continued to work on government projects and was aided greatly by having their regional offices. Like most quantity surveyors they were busy partly because there was so much construction work that needed to be measured and valued but also because there was a shortage of good staff as a result of the war. Langdon, himself was on site on Salisbury Plain for a couple of years; there were offices on the South Coast and in the North-West and Lincolnshire and site offices, including a Fleet Air Arm project at Anthorn in Cumbria. (According to John Laing, the contractor, this was "a beast", partly due to ground conditions and partly due to the weather, 29 days of rain in August 1942!).

Davis Belfield & Everest

Owen Davis came from a middle class family of Welsh origin. He served his articles in the 1920s with his cousin, PT Walters. In his own words, the profession was not easy:

> If you were lucky, your father paid £300 to have you articled for three years and one or two firms cashed in on this and got most of their taking off done for nothing. If you were less lucky, you started off as an office boy at 10 shillings (50 pence) a week. Promotion was slow. Comptometers did not exist and a junior, unless he was articled, might expect to spend years doing little more than squaring, casting and extending; the break-through into working-up was a major event. Office hours automatically included Saturday mornings and in most offices overtime was virtually enforced except at slack periods. Luncheon vouchers and state or office pension schemes were, of course, unheard of and two weeks holiday a year was the maximum for both seniors and juniors.

Some elements of that statement are intelligible to today's reader, particularly if they are quantity surveyors, others are not; others still, like the mention of luncheon vouchers, date it.[7] Davis, perhaps because he was articled to his cousin, did not pay a premium and got paid, 10 shillings (50 pence) per week in the first year, 20 shillings (£1) in the second and 30 shillings (£1.50) in the third.

After completing his articles, Davis, like a number of QSs at the time, turned to 'charing', working on an hourly basis for different firms, while he was completing his professional examinations. On qualification as a Professional Associate of the Surveyors' Institution (PASI), Davis entered a difficult job market. He eventually got employment as a temporary taker-off with Dearle & Henderson but, after a few months, he was asked to prepare a bill of quantities for an architect friend for a small rectory in Brantham.

34 Red Lion Square. Like many of the firms' early premises, the actual building is no longer there; it was redeveloped in the 1960s. The building on the left has also been replaced but the one on the right is still there, only slightly modified.
Copyright Camden Local Studies and Archive Centre.

This job was undertaken satisfactorily and Owen Davis, Chartered Quantity Surveyor, aged 23, was in business. It was 1931.

Davis started in practice at 34 Red Lion Square. He rented a room from PT Walters, his cousin. Early work was mainly domestic and relatively small scale but the practice survived and, despite the market conditions, grew and in 1934 profits were over £600.[8] That year, John Belfield, who had also been articled to Walters, decided to start in practice at the same address. Shortly after, they agreed to enter into partnership as Davis and Belfield, chartered quantity surveyors, and moved to bigger offices in Bedford Row. The two, who had helped each other on projects before, got on well and looked forward to developing a practice together. But it was not to be; less than six months after the partnership was established, John Belfield committed suicide.

The reasons for Belfield's suicide are unclear. There are suggestions that he had been overworking, completing his external examinations with the Surveyors' Institution as well as trying to establish the practice. It has also been suggested that he felt that his contribution to the partnership was not what he would have liked it to be. These are almost certainly not the whole story. Davis records the reason as a nervous breakdown. He insisted on Belfield remaining in the firm's name as it developed over the following 30 odd years that he led it. And, in fact, it stayed for over 50 years until 1988 and the merger with Langdon & Every.

By the late 1930s, Davis & Belfield was busy and successful. Davis was lecturing at the Architectural Association (AA) in London and the Cambridge School of Architecture and writing articles for *The Architects' Journal*. These activities would become the basis of long-standing relationships. Davis mentions Peter Bicknall, who practised in Cambridge for many years; and Richard Llewellyn-Davies and Peter Moro, who he notes found their first clients when they were at the AA. Davis was also close to FRS Yorke, the founder of Yorke, Rosenberg & Mardall (YRM), and Ernö Goldfinger.

During the war, annual fee income varied between £1,500 and £6,000 and profit between £400 and £1,800. Until 1944, Davis was the sole partner.

Bobbie Everest was a successful sole practitioner in his own right. He was two years older than Davis, had qualified in 1928 and started in practice in Hove in the early 1930s while simultaneously doing temporary taking off. In 1937 he moved to an office in Lower Belgrave Street. He was a friend of Davis, they had helped each other out on a number of occasions and there had even been talk of partnership before the war intervened. On the outbreak of war, Everest's clients dispersed and he gave up private practice to become directly involved in war work, largely for the Air Ministry. He apparently ended up living with his family on a houseboat on the Norfolk Broads while acting as chief quantity surveyor for an RAF station at Rackheath, near Norwich. Everest was a great grandson of Sir George Everest, Surveyor General of India, after whom the famous peak was named.[9]

With the outbreak of war in 1939, the firm of Davis & Belfield concentrated on government work: temporary hospitals, aerodromes, military camps and the like for the Admiralty, War Department and Air Ministry. They worked with Richard Sheppard (later of Sheppard Robson) on an emergency hospital at Worksop. Towards the end of the war, the workload switched to repair of war damaged buildings and reconstruction work. They were bombed out of their own office in Bedford Row in 1942, and moved to temporary accomodations in Swiss Cottage.

In 1943 Bobbie Everest gave up his government employment, returned to private practice in London and ended up sharing space with Owen Davis in apartments in Ashley Place in Victoria. In Everest's case he had both home and office in Ashley Place. This led to collaboration and in 1944, agreement to join in partnership as Davis Belfield & Everest (DB&E).

Commentary

The origins of the two firms were rather different. Horace Langdon was older and more experienced and started his firm on the back of his work in, and connections from, the War Department during the First World War. He was also from a relatively modest background and that was unusual in partners in professional firms at the time. Tom Every was more similar to Davis, Belfield and Everest, a middle class, ex-public school boy, the archetypical partner in a professional firm. Every was, of course, not a qualified quantity surveyor, although he was a member of the Surveyors Institution (a prerequisite for being a partner in a firm of chartered surveyors). This was not uncommon, later partners were to be building surveyors, for example, and Nick Davis, Owen's son, qualified as a general practice surveyor.

Both firms got most, if not all, of their work directly or indirectly from architects and it was relationships with architects that they worked on in these early years. That was normal for quantity surveyors. It is only since the Second World War that quantity surveyors and quantity surveying have genuinely been seen as professionals in their own right. In the 1920s and 1930s, they were seen as supporting architects and were often sub-contractors to architects. Quantity surveyors were not credited on projects in the technical press until after the war.

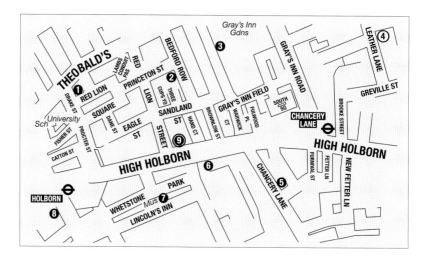

By the 1930s, Langdon and Every were establishment figures in the industry and the community and had a much more established practice than Owen Davis. The people they worked with, clients and architects, were also established. The architects they worked with, for example, Seely & Paget and Grey Wornum, were leading firms of the period.

Davis & Belfield and then Davis Belfield & Everest were favourite quantity surveyors of a number of younger architects of the day. Davis attended meetings at the home of FRS Yorke, before the war and DB&E provided office space for YRM when they were bombed out in the last years of the war; Belfield worked with Godfrey Samuel, later to become a partner in Tecton, in the early 1930s, including a school in Swanage in Dorset; and there are frequent mentions of D&B and DB&E in the Goldfinger archive at the library of the Royal Institute of British Architects (RIBA). It notes DB&E working on the Communist Party Headquarters in Covent Garden at the end of the war and collaboration on a proposed book before the war.

The map above shows the various offices in London of Horace W Langdon & Every up to 1945 and Davis & Belfield up to 1942. It does not show the D&B offices in Swiss Cottage, North London, where they moved to when they were bombed out of their offices in 32 Bedford Row in 1942, or the offices they shared with Bobbie Everest at Ashley Place, Victoria, in 1943 which became the first office of Davis Belfield & Everest when the partnership was formed the following year. The map also shows, in the centre, Davis Langdon's current offices in MidCity Place, High Holborn, and, on the far right, Langdon Buildings in Leather Lane, the Council residential block named after Mayor Horace Langdon.

Map showing significant locations for the firm in Holborn.

1 34 Red Lion Square, Owen Davis
   (1931–1935) and John Belfield (1934).

2 Bedford Row, Davis & Belfield (1935–1942).

3 6 Raymond Buildings, Gray's Inn,
   Horace W Langdon (1919).

4 Langdon Buildings, Leather Lane,
   council residential block named after
   Mayor Horace Langdon (1965).

5 57/58 Chancery Lane,
   Horace W Langdon (1920–1928).

6 292 High Holborn,
   Horace W Langdon & Every (1928–1940).

7 20/23 Lincoln's Inn Fields,
   Horace W Langdon & Every (1940–1942).

8 Kingsway House, 103 Kingsway,
   Horace W Langdon & Every (1942–1954)

9 MidCity Place, 71 High Holborn,
   Davis Langdon LLP (2003–present).

HWL&E were unusual in expanding nationally before the war, and were quick off the mark in their international expansion after the war. They had grown steadily over the previous 20 years or so and clearly intended to continue growing. D&B, and particularly, DB&E, were much smaller and much newer than HWL&E but they also very quickly began to expand nationally. Both firms were poised to profit from a more or less regular flow of work over the next two decades.

1   For example, Gardiner & Theobald and Northcroft Neighbour & Nicholson (now Northcrofts), both founded in 1840, Widnell & Trollope (now Widnells) in 1852 and Gleeds in 1875. EC Harris was founded just before the First World War, in 1911.

2   Local 'standard' methods of measurement had been in existence for many years; this was the first national method, applicable to England.

3   Holloways was taken over by John Laing & Co in 1964. Laing, in turn was taken over in 2001 to become Laing O'Rourke.

4   Patterson & Kempster, the forerunner of Davis Langdon PKS in Dublin, also recorded work on similar compensation claims at the same time.

5   Langdon's wife's family was local to Romford and that may have been a source of this work.

6   Bradford & Bingley's retail deposit accounts and branch network were transferred to Abbey, part of Santander, in 2008; the rest of the business was taken into public ownership.

7   Written in 1969, the 25th anniversary of Davis Belfield & Everest, and published in *DB&E News*, Edition 6.

8   Equivalent to £25,680 in 2008, using the Retail Price Index.

9   Everest (1790–1866) was Surveyor General of India from 1829–1843 and the mountain was named after him by his successor, AS Waugh in 1856.

Chapter Three

After the War

The first 25 years after the Second World War was a period of almost continuous growth in the construction industry. The graph below shows construction output in constant 2000 prices from 1955 to 1970.[1] Over the period, output doubled in real terms (an average annual rate of almost five per cent) and indicates more or less steady growth, although there is the beginning of a downturn at the end of the 1960s. The graph can be compared with the graphs on page 57 (1970–1990) and page 118 (1988–2003), which are compiled on the same basis and drawn to the same scale. The complete graph from 1955 to 2008 appears on page 193.

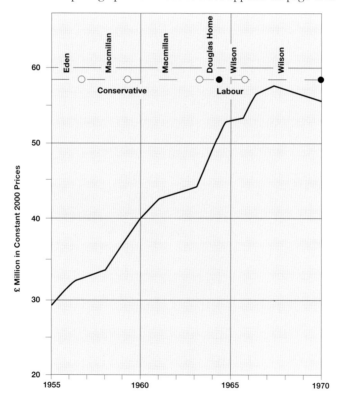

Graph showing construction output by all agencies, 1955 to 1970. Source: Office for National Statistics (ONS).

The government planning that had been undertaken during the war (including the Beveridge Report on the welfare state and the Simon Report on construction) was to continue after the war was over. There was a belief that central planning and scientific method were the means of achieving the desired social and economic objectives. As a result, the public sector was not only the regulator of the construction industry but a major client. New public sector construction output as a proportion of total output was 50 per cent in 1955 and 46 per cent in 1970; it was 25 per cent in 2000.

Immediately after the war, the focus of the British government's efforts was on essential repair and reconstruction and this lasted for a number of years but attention and investment soon transferred to large scale new developments that were to keep the industry busy through the 1950s and 1960s. The agenda of the Labour governments (1945–1951 and 1964–1967) was to transform British society and building homes, factories, schools, hospitals and universities was a central part of that. The Conservative government was more concerned with Britain's role in the world but still competed with Labour to invest in public buildings, particularly, housing and schools. Between 1945 and 1970, public housing completions averaged 165,000 units per year, 57 per cent of all completions.

Private sector developers were initially constrained by the need for building licences and other regulations and an acute shortage of building materials, and there was very little new commercial development between 1945 and 1950. Because of the shortage of new warehouse, retail and office space, property prices rose rapidly creating an environment for property investment and a number of major developers, including Land Securities and Hammersons, were founded at this time. In 1951 a Conservative government replaced the Labour government that had been elected immediately after the war, and in 1954 building licence restrictions were removed. This resulted in a major property boom from 1955 to 1964.

In 1964, a Labour government, headed by Harold Wilson was returned and, despite major economic problems, pressed ahead with public investment in buildings. This included the new universities and hospital building programmes that helped to keep firms like Langdon & Every (L&E) and Davis Belfield & Everest (DB&E) busy into the 1970s.

The Ministry of Housing and Local Government and the Ministry of Public Building and Works, and client ministries like Education and Health, employed large numbers of professionals, architects, engineers and quantity surveyors, to help government set and implement policy. With the professional institutions and private practitioners, they set standards and procedures and produced design guides and cost limits. Quantity surveyors were heavily involved in all of this, particularly the last.

The 1960s saw the development of tender price indices and cost analysis and the establishment of cost planning and the Building Cost Information Service (BCIS) of the Royal Institution of Chartered Surveyors (RICS). The RICS concluded that the distinctive competence of the QS was "skill in measurement and valuation in the field of construction in order that such work can be described and the cost and price be forecast, analysed, planned, controlled and accounted for".[2] This was much more than the production of bills of quantities and the preparation of interim and final accounts. Not all firms of quantity surveyors took to these new roles but both L&E and DB&E were heavily involved in industry bodies and the new developments; partners in both firms were active in the RICS, the BCIS, the Building Research Establishment, the Joint Contracts Tribunal and other bodies.

Langdon & Every

In early 1946, Tom Every returned to L&E from his secondment at the Ministry of Works and later that year received a CBE in the New Years Honours list for his services during the war. The firm quickly became involved in post-war reconstruction work. Every's senior position in government paid dividends, contacts were consolidated, work flowed in and the practice flourished. On his return, a second office was taken at 22 Russell Square in Bloomsbury, in addition to Kingsway House, and the firm was to maintain and extend that office for a further 17 years. The building was leased from the University of London and on the ground floor was the Registrar of Births, Marriages and Deaths for Holborn Council. For many years, the younger staff in the firm did a good trade in acting as marriage witnesses, for a fee, of course.

Open to new markets, the partners took advantage of two significant overseas opportunities in 1946. After the war, two former employees, Frank Angell and Eric Watson, had found their way back to London and jobs with HWL&E. They had practiced as Waters, Watson & Angell in Singapore in the 1930s and within a few months, they were thinking of returning to the Far East but could not afford to do so without support.[3] They approached Tom Every and he encouraged them to return to Singapore as local partners of a new firm, Horace W Langdon & Every (Far East). They jumped at the chance. Initially, work for that office came largely from the public sector, either directly from Colonial Government in London or locally from the Public Works Department. A couple of years later offices were opened in Kuala Lumpur, also in colonial Malaya, and Hong Kong, both before 1950. The Far East branch of the firm was established.

Also in 1946, Tom Every received a telephone call from an old colleague from the early days of his war work, JM Wilson. "Would Every like to go out to Persia at once to write a report on their proposed programme of work in Abadan and the oil fields for the Anglo-Iranian Oil Company (AIOC)?"[4] The prompt answer was "Of course." Apparently the quantity surveyor AIOC had appointed had refused to travel by air and would only go by sea and that would take weeks. The next day, Every had his medical, was given his inoculations and in no time was on his way to Iran in a converted

Lancaster bomber. In retrospect, these decisions to go to the Far East and the Middle East were to have far reaching consequences. The development of the firm's offices internationally is described in "Chapter Six".

In 1949, Langdon was 70 and a celebratory lunch was held for over 150 people at the Connaught Rooms in Great Queen Street. Some of the guests would, no doubt, have been family or friends but the number suggests that HWL&E was a substantial firm by this time. The table layout identifies representatives from the Kingsway and Russell Square offices in London and from regional offices in Liverpool and Stoke on Trent, in the North-West, and Plymouth, Southampton and Portsmouth, on the South Coast. The top table, in addition to Langdon and Every and their wives, has Langdon's daughter and her husband, a young Giles Every, Tom's son and a future senior partner, Eric Watson from Singapore, Aubrey Lawrence, partnership secretary and Ivan Lankester, the office manager. Lankester proposed the toast to the senior partner. John Porter and Reg Brooks, also future partners of the firm, headed two of the other tables. There were 14 members of the RICS indicated on the seating plan, perhaps, a sign that the designation was deemed significant and that a firm of chartered quantity surveyors of the time did not have a high proportion of qualified staff.

From 1947 there were regular visits by Langdon and Every to the Far East offices and, early in the 1950s, Giles Every visited Singapore. Langdon's visits were grand affairs. The journey was by sea and took six weeks each way so the whole thing would take some months. In addition, there would be side trips on RICS business or for Masonic events or for golf. In Singapore

From left to right, Frank Angell, Tom Every, Horace Langdon, Aubrey Lawrence and Eric Watson, in Kingsway House, 1947.

there would be receptions and cocktail parties. Although the London office assisted with recruitment for overseas posts, there was very little exchange of staff. In the early days, John Winship was sent from Southampton to help out for a few months in Singapore but this kind of transfer was uncommon.

Nothing is known of the partnership agreement between Langdon and Every except that, following the problems with Taylor in the 1920s, it was almost certainly short and simple. They had a very prudent approach to financing the firm: it was largely run on retained profits (partners did not draw all their earnings) and retired partners' capital (on which they were paid interest) and did not involve bank overdrafts. Capital shares were relatively low so a large share of the firm's capital was not necessarily a lot of money.

While this approach had a number of advantages, it had the effect of removing a direct relationship between a year's profit and the partners' incomes in that year. In a steady market, this did not matter much but in a rising or falling market it could lead to disconnects; it could also have an effect in the event of windfall income. The L&E partners used the term "on the bus and off the bus" to describe the acceptance that partners took the effects of their, and their predecessors', actions as they fell.

Horace Langdon's celebratory lunch for his 70th birthday, the Connaught Rooms, 1949.

Horace Langdon died on 9 November 1954, aged 75. He had been involved, although not on active service, in two World Wars and seen his firm grow from a sole practitioner in Gray's Inn to one of the largest quantity surveying practices in the UK and, almost certainly, the largest international practice. His obituary in the *RICS Journal* listed many of his achievements in the profession and more widely. He was elected to the QS Committee of the Surveyors Institution in 1927 and had been a member of the Council of the Institution since 1936. On his death, the Kingsway office was closed and Aubrey Lawrence and his staff moved to an office in Bedford Row. In 1955, the "Horace W" was dropped and the firm became simply Langdon & Every.

Possibly in preparation for Langdon's death or retirement, John Porter had been made a partner the previous year but he would have been relatively junior, so the bulk of the firm was then owned by Tom Every with, probably, an annuity to Langdon's widow. Thereafter, we know that partners' shares were determined by the most senior partners of the day. Latterly, the Langdon & Every partners' official retirement age was 65, although Langdon died as a partner, aged 75 and Every retired at 61. On retirement, retired partners and their widows received annuities until their death.

After Langdon's death, new UK partners did not participate in the overseas ventures. From 1954, the UK shares in the Far East and Middle East were held by Tom Every. The Far East shares were, of course, declining (in percentage terms, if not in value) as local partners took increasing ownership of the offices in South-East Asia. When Every retired ten years later, his shares in the Far East and the Middle East were passed to his son, Giles. Generally, when a partner died or retired, his shares were taken up by the continuing partners.

From 1948 to 1955, the firm had an overflow office at 292 High Holborn, above the Holborn Empire (demolished in 1960 and now the site of Blackwell's bookshop, near Holborn tube station), apparently where work for the Middle East was done. In 1952, they purchased a lease on 21 Russell Square, adjacent to 22 and most of the firm moved from Kingsway House.[5] Only Langdon and Lawrence, the company secretary, and some administrative staff stayed at Kingsway. The two buildings in Russell Square were connected and extensively altered.

John Porter, based in London, was the first 'second generation' partner. He was in his early 40s and had been with the firm since 1935, mainly in London but, during the war, had been based in a number of the UK offices. Reg Brooks, who had been resident partner in Southampton, since 1951 when John Winship had died, was invited to join the UK partnership and move to

London in 1956. He was around 50. At the same time, Frank Angell returned from Singapore and replaced Brooks in Southampton.

Immediately after the war, HWL&E was working largely with architects and client contacts that they had had before or during the war. They had also acquired a number of clients through Tom Every's government work. They worked with Seely & Paget on war damage and improvements at Westminster Abbey, Lambeth Palace, St George's Chapel and St Paul's Cathedral. In 1947, the first resident surveyor was installed at Ascot racecourse, a post that was to be filled by the firm for the next five decades.

In 1953 HWL&E was appointed quantity surveyors to the Harlow New Town Development Corporation and an office was opened, originally in a site hut. The masterplanner for Harlow was Sir Frederick Gibberd & Partners and the firm worked with them and with the New Town Development Corporation staff and other firms of architects. Colin Brearley recalls housing projects with Norman & Dawbarn in the 1960s. The office was active until the early 1980s, latterly sharing space with Gibberds.

In 1959, Tom Every started preparing for his retirement and bought a farm in Chagford in Devon. In 1961, his son Giles became a partner and, when Every senior retired at the age of 61 in 1963, three new partners were appointed, Colin Brearley, Ken Maclean and Dick Holmes. The new partners decided to query Every on the proposed partnership arrangements but were brusquely informed that the offer was non-negotiable. These three joined John Porter, Reg Brooks and Giles Every as UK partners.

The Langdon & Every offices in Russell Square in the 1960s, Nos. 21 and 22 are second and third from left and the building has an attic storey.

Colin Brearley had been with the firm in London since the 1950s; Dick Holmes had been in Hong Kong for many years; and Ken Maclean had been in the Middle East; the last two had only relatively recently returned to the UK. Jim Driscoll joined the UK partnership in 1968, having been a partner in the Middle East.

Tom Every had a government appointment as cost adviser to the Horse Racing Levy Board and this was inherited by Colin Brearley. The position involved advising on the costs of developments that were put forward for grants to be funded by the Levy. There were around 50 racecourses of all types so the job was large as well as prestigious. Another cost adviser had to be used when L&E were appointed as executive quantity surveyors and, interestingly, Hugh Tunbridge, an associate of DB&E, was that adviser.

In the 1960s L&E were quantity surveyors on a number of well-know headquarters office buildings, including the Daily Mirror building at Holborn Circus, designed by Anderson Forster & Wilcox with Owen Williams & Partners, completed in 1960 and demolished in the 1990s to make way for Sainsbury's new headquarters; Brittanic House in Moorgate for BP, designed by Milton Cashmore & Partners, completed in 1967 and revamped in 2000 by Sheppard Robson; and, at the end of the decade, the Commercial Union (CU) Assurance and P&O Steamship buildings in Leadenhall Street, both designed by Gollins Melvin Ward (GMW). The CU Assurance building was the tallest hung frame building in the world at the time and the first building in the City of London to be taller than St Paul's Cathedral; it was damaged by a terrorist bomb in 1992 and completely re-clad to replicate the appearance, but upgrade the performance, of the original. The P&O building was demolished, top down, in 2007 to make way for Richard Rogers 48 floor, 225 metre tall Leadenhall building. In the 1990s, Davis Langdon worked on the refurbishment of the CU building and was appointed as cost manager on the Leadenhall building.

Headquarters buildings were not limited to the UK. In the 1960s, HWL&E were responsible for BP country head offices in Tehran, and Melbourne. The latter, originally designed by Demaine Russell Armstrong Orton and Trundle, was converted to apartments in the 1990s.

Also in the 1960s, L&E worked on the redevelopment of Euston Station, designed by Richard Siefert; on a series of power stations for the Atomic Energy Authority and the Central Electricity Generating Board; the development of Chelsea Barracks for the Brigade of Guards, designed by Tripe & Wakeham; and town centre developments at Lewisham and Harlow. Other projects included new grandstands at Ascot, a Design and

Top: The Daily Mirror building at Holborn Circus, Anderson Forster & Wilcox with Owen Williams & Partners.
Bottom: Brittanic House for British Petroleum, Milton Cashmore & Partners

Build project by George Wimpey, and Doncaster, designed by HV Lobb and Partners; these latter projects flowed from the firm's Betting Levy Board appointment.

Public buildings included hospitals for the Wessex Regional Hospital Board, United Liverpool Hospitals, the South-West Regional Hospital Board and Middlesex Hospital Medical School; university buildings at Liverpool, Manchester, Edinburgh, London and Birmingham universities, and projects for the Army and the Air Force all over the country.

At the end of the 1960s, Langdon & Every had around 300 people in the UK in ten offices. There were over 100 staff in London; the largest offices outside London were in the North-West with 80 staff in three offices (Liverpool, Chester and Manchester); and there were 50 staff in site offices around the country. There were ten people in Langdon & Every (Arabian Gulf), mainly in Bahrain, and around 80 in Langdon Every & Seah in Singapore, Hong Kong, Malaysia and Brunei.

Davis Belfield & Everest

The partnership of Davis Belfield & Everest was established in Ashley Place in Victoria when the war ended with Owen Davis and Bobbie Everest as the two partners; Davis was 38 in 1945, Everest, 40. Peter Mill returned from war service in 1945 and became a partner in 1946, aged 33 (partnership had been discussed in the late 1930s but the war intervened). John Parrinder joined the firm in 1947 and became a partner in 1949, aged 34. These four were to comprise a first generation of partners and see the firm through the 1950s.

Repair and reconstruction work continued for some time after the war and was the rationale for DB&E's first office outside London but the interesting post-war work came via the architects that Owen Davis, in particular, had spent time with in the 1930s, including FRS Yorke and Ernö Goldfinger. In this period the firm also became involved with construction research and publishing. In 1944, DB&E was appointed to provide a technical advisory service for *The Architects' Journal* and, in 1947, they took over the editorship of *Spon's Architects' and Builders' Price Book*. Owen Davis and Peter Mill taught at the Architectural Association and the Department of Architecture at Cambridge. John Parrinder was chair of the Building Research Establishment.

In 1946, the firm opened its first branch offices in Norwich and Newport. Norwich was established to work on air fields in East Anglia; Newport was established to work on the Brynmawr factory, a government initiated industrial investment in South Wales. DB&E were appointed for work on the Atomic Weapons Research Establishment at Aldermaston in 1950 and work there continued into the 1960s.

DB&E's work in the City of London in the 1950s was very different from the work that the firm is engaged in 50 years later, partly because priorities and the general pattern of work were very different but also because the firm's focus was different. Their two major projects were publicly funded, by the City, and were basically housing projects. They were also designed by the same firm of architects. The first, Golden Lane, was the result of a design competition in 1951 won by Geoffrey Powell and this success was the origin of the firm of Chamberlin Powell & Bon. The development was built between 1952 and 1961. At the time of the Golden Lane competition, the three partners were teaching at Kingston Polytechnic; all were in their early 30s; all had submitted entries for the Golden Lane competition; and they had agreed to form a partnership if one of them won.

In the mid-1950s, Chamberlin Powell & Bon were invited by the City to design the adjacent Barbican development, 14 hectares of largely bombed out wasteland north of Gresham Street.

Chamberlin Powell & Bon were the kind of architects that Owen Davis and his partners tended to encourage when they were approached to help on projects. It was partly because they liked working with interesting young designers but also because they believed that such designers often became successful established design practices. And quantity surveyors' work at the time still came largely via, if not directly from, architects. The attraction of DB&E to the young architects was that they were tolerant, supportive and imaginative and brought substantial practical experience to projects. Many years later, when a young surveyor's estimate for a Chamberlin Powell & Bon project was being checked by a partner, the latter asked where the allowance for the fountain was. On being told that there was no fountain on the drawing, the young surveyor was gently told that that did not matter, there would be one.

DB&E's work on the Barbican was to continue for three decades and, like all their work at the time, they didn't compete for the work, they were just asked, and it was on scale fees. It is said that Peter Mill was asked at lunch one day if he would like to help with a new housing project in the City. He said "of course" and the job was the Barbican. Work on the Barbican was not only done in London but was farmed out to regional offices and kept parts of the firm busy for many years. Construction work on the buildings started in 1963 and the Barbican development, complete with the Arts Centre, the City

of London School for Girls and the Guildhall School of Music was finally finished in 1981. DB&E had been working on the project for more than quarter of a century when the final account was agreed.

By the end of the 1950s, DB&E had five offices, in London, Belfast, Leeds, Newport and Norwich, and the site office at Aldermaston. Total turnover was £249,272 and total profit before tax £77,002.[6] Each of the four London partners had a 25 per cent share in the business and each earned £19,250 in the year ending 30 April 1959.[7] Turnover had been £20,839 and profit, £7,702 in 1945; they had both increased by an average of roughly 17.5 per cent per annum from the end of the war to the end of the 1950s, a stunning growth rate.

The Barbican Development for the City of London, Chamberlin Powell & Bon. Photographer: Richard Einzig/arcaid.co.uk.

Although the firm did not have offices overseas, they did some work in the Middle East. In the early 1950s, they produced bills of quantities for neighbourhood units in Kuwait and provided staff secondments to Caltex, an American oil company. Owen Davis noted that "the partners never had time to chase work overseas although they were not averse to it if it came along". DB&E also had international links in Australia and South Africa. In Australia, a joint venture was established with Rawlinsons, Davis Belfield & Rawlinson, and there was an Australian edition of *Spon's Price Book* from 1966 (still published) but no joint projects were undertaken. In South Africa, there was a link with Farrow Laing McKechnie which involved staff exchanges but, again, no projects. After the merger with L&E, the Rawlinson's link was broken because DLS had a joint venture company in Sydney (Langdon Every Hunt & Beattie). The Farrow Laing link, however, was maintained and eventually led, via Davis Langdon Farrow Laing, to Davis Langdon Africa and now Davis Langdon.

In 1960/1961, echoing Horace Langdon in the 1930s, Bobbie Everest was elected Mayor of Westminster. He had been a councillor since 1948 and stood down from the council in 1963.

With the firm going from strength to strength and the original partners getting older, the partners began to think about the next generation. The first new partner was Bill Fussell, fresh from running a regional office in Zimbabwe (then Northern Rhodesia) for Northcroft Neighbour & Nicholson. He joined, unusually, directly as a partner, in 1961, aged 35. Fussell was followed by Dick Milborne in 1964. Milborne had worked in the firm for 12 years after full time study. Both Fussell and Milborne had served in the military during the war, Fussell in the Royal Engineers, Milborne in the Royal Air Force.

Three more partners joined in the 1960s: Nick Davis (1966), Owen's son, who joined the firm in 1965 after extended post-university international travels, including spells of work with Farrow Laing, in Johannesburg and Rawlinsons, in Sydney; Geoff Trickey (1967), who had been with the firm, left and was invited back as a partner; and Clyde Malby (1969), who had been with DB&E since 1960. Davis was 26 when he became a partner, Trickey 32 and Malby 34. Another of Owen's sons, Simon, was originally intended to join the firm but chose architecture instead. By the end of the 1960s, therefore, there were nine partners in London.

While Davis was decidedly middle class (and had been to public school and Cambridge University), Trickey and Malby both came from more ordinary backgrounds. Prior to the 1960s, the typical partner in a professional firm was middle class and public school and had family links with other partners, but the 1960s brought a more meritocratic approach to career progression. The same was happening in other professional firms, including L&E and client organisations. Reasons included better educational opportunities for working class people but also a concern that the firm should move with the times having partners from only one class was not only outdated but bad business.

In around 1968, before Malby became a partner, with a partnership of eight and the founding partners shortly to retire, partnership arrangements were becoming complex. A sub-committee of two, Owen Davis, the longest serving, and Geoff Trickey, the most recent partner, were delegated to come up with proposals. They addressed three main issues: profit sharing arrangements, retirement and financial arrangements on retirement.

As noted previously, the four initial partners had equal shares by 1960 although their progresion to that had been rather erratic. New partners joining the practice took shares from the existing partners and this, and subsequent progression, tended to be done in an *ad hoc* way. A typical new partner's share could be as little as, say, three per cent compared to a top partner's share of 20 to 25 per cent; the actual percentage in each case would be discussed and agreed by the partners of the day. Davis and Trickey proposed that new partners would come in on a fixed proportion of a top partner's share and then rise over six or so years to a top partner's, or 'plateau', share. This pattern of shares was reviewed every three years which led, on occasion, to protracted discussions.

In 1968, the oldest partners, Everest and Davis were 63 and 61 respectively so the question of retirement was pressing. The proposal was that Davis, Everest, Mill and Parrinder would retire at 65 and that, thereafter, partners would retire at 60. Davis and Trickey were both conscious of the need to encourage the aspirations of younger people and address the problem of older partners 'hanging on'. All of the initial partners stepped down progressively in their last years as a partner, one day per week each year. Owen Davis did this and was very strict about the days he came into the office and would not change them even to accommodate 'important meetings'.

The final issue Davis and Trickey addressed was post-retirement partnership arrangements. It was agreed that no work should be undertaken by a retired partner that conflicted with partnership interests and that any work should be cleared with the continuing partners. Retired partners could withdraw their capital in the business over a five year period and that amount would be what they had put into the business over their years as a partner. Unlike L&E, DB&E distributed profits in the year they were earned and, while they had substantial partners' funds as working capital, they also used bank overdrafts.

The partnership was assumed to have no value, no good-will. On retirement, partners received a 'consultancy' for five years. The amount of this was based

on their last three years earnings and was typically a third of the annual average of the three years.

The proposals were all adopted and became the basis of DB&E's and subsequently DL&E's partnership arrangements until recently. The 1988 merger established an incoming partner's share as a fixed 37.5 per cent of a plateau partner's share, rising by 12.5 per cent increments to 100 per cent after six years. Age discrimination legislation threatened the fixed retirement age in 2007; consultancies were abandoned in 2008; and the One Firm One Future restructuring in 2008 affected all the arrangements, though they had served the firm well for 40 years.[8]

These management and organisational arrangements were developed for, and applied in, the London office. In the branches, local partners started with a minority share (typically 30 per cent) in their branch and, over time that share increased. In the 1960s, the local share never exceeded 50 per cent but later it could be 70 per cent or more, probably by that stage shared among a number of local partners.

The volume and range of DB&E's workload in the 1960s was extensive and nationwide. It included housing, arts buildings, churches, universities, schools, hospitals, industrial and office buildings and involved working with the leading design firms of the day. There were major housing projects for the Greater London Council in Hackney, Bermondsey, designed by Yorke Rosenberg Mardall (YRM) and built using a Wates System. Southwark Borough Architects designed 64 acres (25 hectares) of Southwark for housing using Laing's 12M Jesperson System, the Aylesbury Estate (soon to be demolished). This was the heyday of industrialised, system built, mainly heavy concrete panel, often high-rise housing, brought to a dramatic halt by the collapse of Ronan Point in Newham, East London, in 1968.[9] Other iconic housing projects included Trellick Towers in Goldhawk Road, North Kensington, designed by Ernö Goldfinger. This last building is now Grade II listed and, in 2007, one bedroom flats sold for £250,000 and three bedroom flats for £465,000.

There were university buildings at Leeds, designed by Chamberlin Powell & Bon, at Imperial College, designed by the Architects Co-Partnership, at Cambridge designed by Gollins Melvin Ward (GMW), at Oxford, designed by Howell Killick, Partridge & Amis (HKPA) and at East Anglia, designed by Denys Lasdun. The last was, of course, one of the new universities, famous for its ziggurat residential blocks.

Trellick Towers, London, Ernö Goldfinger.
Photograph: Gevin Jackson/arcaid.co.uk.

Arts and social buildings included the National Theatre with Denys Lasdun & Partners. A 1966 *DB&E News* noted that this project was still 'Secret'

(suggesting that *DB&E News* was very much an internal publication). Work was starting on the Barbican Arts Centre, Ipswich Civic Centre, designed by Vine & Vine, the Old Vic Theatre in Bristol, the Playhouse Theatre in Nottingham, designed by Peter Moro & Partners, and the Odeon Cinema at the Elephant & Castle. In one *DB&E News* there was a cryptic mention of a "theatre for a well known public school"; a later edition refers to a new hall at Eton, designed by AM Gear.

School buildings included St Paul's School, Barnes, designed by Fielding & Mawson, using the CLASP steel frame system.[10]

There were hospitals in Hillingdon and Kettering designed by GMW, Princess Margaret, Swindon and Wythenshawe, designed by Powell & Moya, John Radcliffe, Oxford and Wakefield, designed by YRM, West Cheshire, designed by the Architects Fellowship and Charing Cross Hospital at Fulham in West London, designed by Ralph Tubbs. One of the *DB&E News* noted modestly that "We have acted as quantity surveyors on most of the hospitals designed by YRM and on three out of four hospitals designed by Powell & Moya."

Office buildings included the International Wool Secretariat at Ilkley, designed by Chippindale & Edmondson and a headquarters building for the South Wales Electricity Board designed by GMW. The latter comprised 122,263 square feet and had an approximate cost of one million pounds.

Commentary

Both firms grew steadily in the post-war period. It was a good time for the construction industry and for quantity surveyors. There was more or less steady demand from the public sector for public housing, schools, hospitals, university buildings and the like and larger private clients commissioned headquarters buildings. Both firms were heavily involved in all types of public work; L&E was also responsible for a number of corporate headquarters buildings in the UK and overseas.

The post-war period saw the transition of both firms from the founding partners to a second generation of partners. The diagram overleaf shows the evolution of the partnerships from two or three partner practices after the war, to three or four partners in the late 1950s, to seven to nine partners in the late 1960s. The 1960s also saw the end of partners in both firms being selected from a single social class. The partnerships were small by today's standards but actually rather large for the time. L&E's practice of taking partners from the

Top left: Charing Cross Hospital, London, Ralph Tubbs.
Top right: St Anthony's College, Oxford, Howell Killick, Partridge & Amis.
Centre: John Radcliffe Hospital, Oxford, Yorke Rosenberg & Mardall.
Bottom: The National Theatre, London, Denys Lasdun & Partners.

overseas firms into the UK partnership was an unusual form of recruitment that occasionally created some resentment from senior staff in the UK.

Both Tom Every and Owen Davis had sons that joined their firms. That was not at all unusual for professional firms in the nineteenth and early twentieth centuries, they were family, as well as professional, firms. There were numbers of Gardiner's and Theobald's in Gardiner & Theobald and generations of Harris' in EC Harris & Partners. Interestingly, neither Giles Every nor Nick Davis studied quantity surveying at university but did eventually succumb to either the temptation or the pressure to join the family firm.

	1945		1950		1955		1960		1965		1970
Horace W Langdon & Every (1925–1955)/Langdon & Every (1955–1988)											
HW Langdon											
CT Every											
JH Porter											
RAE Brooks											
G Every											
CC Brearley											
CR Holmes											
KA Maclean											
AW Berryman											
JA Driscoll											
MA McLeod											
Davis Belfield & Everest (1944–1988)											
OA Davis											
RL Everest											
SF Mill											
ER Parrinder											
WFJ Fussell											
RAE Milborne											
NA Davis											
GG Trickey											
CC Malby											

Diagram showing the partners in L&E and DB&E from the end of the war until 1970 (it is continued on page 70).

In the early 1970s, the Quantity Surveyors Divisional Council of the RICS commissioned *A Study of Quantity Surveying Practice* "to provide an informed analysis of the current state of the quantity surveyor's art in order subsequently to determine the ability of the profession to satisfy the emergent demands on it", providing a useful snapshot of the profession in the late 1960s. It described a typical large firm in private practice as comprising more than 50 people, with a maximum of 200 people; it would probably have its head office in London and was most likely established before 1939. Other features included a primary engagement with traditional quantity surveying work; it would be appointed directly for its work, not by architects; and it would have some experience in the use of computers. This description fitted both DB&E and L&E at the time.

Interestingly, the report gives the incidence of university degrees among partners and staff as minimal but around seven per cent of firms had partners or staff who taught regularly and a further 12 per cent who gave occasional lectures. These characteristics ring true for DB&E and L&E; Giles Every and Nick Davis, the youngest partners in their respective firms both had university degrees and many of the partners in both firms lectured.

The system of architectural patronage that had prevailed for most of the twentieth century was beginning to break down in the 1960s and quantity surveyors were increasingly appointed direct by clients. Architectural recommendation or veto, however was still very important. DB&E, in particular, maintained a policy of encouraging and supporting young architects, a policy that demonstrably paid dividends.

1   Construction statistics as we know them today only started in the 1950s, hence this output series starts in 1955. The smooth trend line at the beginning of the series may be a result of the relatively simple price deflators used. Reliable tender price indices and, therefore, price deflators were not developed until the 1960s.

2   *The Future Role of the Quantity Surveyor*, RICS, published in 1971 but commenting on practice in the 1960s. This title was to be used again in *QS 2000, The Future Role of the Quantity Surveyor*, published in 1991 and produced by Davis Langdon Consultancy.

3   Watson was captured by the Japanese and spent his war years in Thailand on the Burma Railway; Waters was taken to Japan and died there; and Angell served in the Royal Engineers.

4   AIOC became British Petroleum (BP) in 1954.

5   The terrace, in the North-West corner of Russell Square, was reduced in length (at No. 21) when the Institute of Education was built in Bedford Way in the late 1960s.

6   £249,272 is equivalent to £4.36 million in 2008, using the Retail Price Index (RPI).

7   £19,250 is equivalent to £336,480, again using the RPI.

8   "One Firm One Future" is discussed in more detail in "Chapter Ten".

9   Shortly after residents had moved in, a gas explosion demolished a load-bearing wall, causing the progressive collapse of one entire corner of the building. Four people were killed and 17 injured.

10   CLASP stands for the Consortium of Local Authorities Special Programme.

Chapter Four

End of the Old Order

The graph opposite shows construction output in constant 2000 prices through the 1970s and 1980s.[1] It clearly shows a declining trend in the 1970s, punctuated by two peaks, in 1973 and 1979, followed by slumps. It was not until 1987 that output returned to 1973 levels. The 1980s, on the other hand, show steady growth from 1981 to 1990 when, of course, there was to be another major downturn.

As the graph indicates, the 1970s was a turbulent decade. There were four general elections: the first, in July 1970, brought a Conservative victory for Edward Heath over Harold Wilson and the last, in May 1979, brought another Conservative victory, this time for Margaret Thatcher over Jim Callaghan, Wilson's successor. The Heath government lasted only four years; Mrs Thatcher's victory led to 18 years of Conservative administrations and a transformation of British society and the British economy. In the two decades, there were 15 years of Conservative government and five of Labour.

The Political and Economic Context

The three priorities of Edward Heath in 1970 were to reorganise government, to address the economy, partly by cuts in public expenditure, and to reform industrial relations. By the end of the year, the Department of Trade and Industry and the Department of the Environment (DoE) had been created, the latter from three ministries, Housing and Local Government, Transport and Public Building and Works. The DoE was, therefore, the main department as far as construction was concerned, as policy maker, regulator and customer.

The economy and labour relations were not so straight-forward. Inflation had begun to emerge as a serious issue after the devaluation of sterling in 1967. Between 1970 and 1973, it averaged over 8.5 per cent and government decided to attempt to regulate prices and incomes. Needless to say, the unions were unenthusiastic and an already strained relationship between the Conservative government and the trade unions was compounded. In 1972, the coal miners went on strike. After some violent incidents, this was settled but a dock strike followed, which was also settled but both settlements undermined the government's credibility.

1973 was a turning point. It started with the UK joining the European Union in January, along with the Republic of Ireland and Denmark. Later in the year, however, national matters came to a head with another confrontation with the miners over pay policy and the aftermath of the

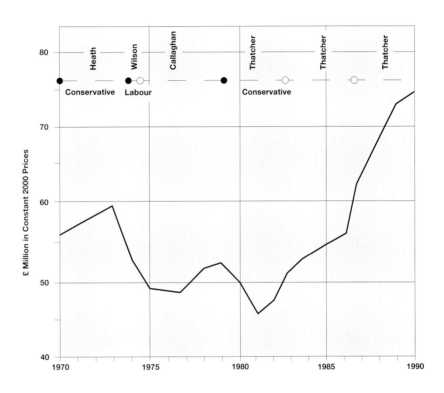

Graph showing all construction output from 1970 to 1990. Source: Office for National Statistics (ONS).

Arab Israeli War of October 1973. The miners introduced an overtime ban, oil imports were restricted by the producers and price increases led to a fourfold increase in the oil import bill. On 13 November the government declared a state of emergency: electricity was only provided to industry on three specified days a week, a 50 miles per hour speed limit was imposed and there was a maximum heating limit on all commercial premises. In February 1974, Heath called the second general election of the 1970s and the result was a hung parliament. Labour had four more seats than the Conservatives but the balance of power was held by the 37 seats of the minority parties.

Harold Wilson became Prime Minister in March 1974 and within days the miners' strike was settled and the three day week and the state of emergency came to an end. However, the government needed a real mandate and a second election was called in October 1974. Although Labour did not win an overall majority they had 40 seats more than the Conservatives. Inflation, however, continued to be a problem, between 1974 and 1975 it was over 20 per cent, and from 1975 there was a compulsory wages' policy. Wilson, unexpectedly, resigned in 1976 and, after a leadership election, Jim Callaghan became Prime Minister in April 1976.

In the same year there was a currency crisis and the government was forced to go to the International Monetary Fund for a loan. As a result there were simultaneous increases in taxation and cuts in public expenditure. This marked a low point in the economy and, thereafter, conditions started improving, assisted by revenues from North Sea oil which were starting to come on-stream. But the Labour government was finally to come to grief on the 1978/1979 'winter of discontent'. This started with a national lorry drivers' strike seeking a 25 per cent wage increase. Industrial unrest spread to public services, including ambulance workers and dustmen.

It is difficult to sort economic and industrial trends tidily into periods but, generally, the UK economy, society and the construction industry were all in a state of flux at the beginning of the 1980s. The country had emerged rather battered from the turmoil of the 1970s that had culminated in the election of Margaret Thatcher in May 1979. The election was a watershed. It returned a Conservative government with a working majority and the first British female Prime Minister. Their first budget cut income tax, raised VAT, reduced public spending and abolished controls on prices and incomes. It also introduced monetarism and targeting the money supply, and most importantly, a belief in the market.

By 1982, inflation was back to single figures but unemployment was still high, over three million. The government was determined to reduce public expenditure and this was to be achieved by a freeze on public sector pay and recruitment, pressure on the nationalised industries to become (more) profitable and an efficiency drive in Whitehall. So far as the nationalised industries were concerned, the ultimate solution was privatisation and this was pushed from the early 1980s.

Mrs Thatcher also had local authorities and trade unions in her sights. The main area for cuts in public expenditure was housing. Social housing completions by local authorities and housing associations fell from over 100,000 to less than 50,000 between 1979 and 1982. Council rents were increased and sitting tenants were encouraged by discounts of up to 50 per cent to buy their homes; between 1979 and 1983, half a million households did.

An election was called in 1983 after the Falklands War and the Conservatives won again with a substantially increased majority. The number and pace of privatisation increased and there were further attempts to reduce the power of the unions. The year-long miners' strike from March 1984 and the government response to it led to serious legislative curbs on the power of the unions.

The Industrial and Professional Context

The 1970s were turbulent years for quantity surveyors working in the commercial property market, with a major boom followed by a major bust in 1973/1974, coinciding with the oil price hike and the three day week. In fact, the boom and bust was largely caused by a massive increase in lending to developers, relaxation of government controls on office development permits and stagnant demand for office space. There was another smaller boom and bust in 1979. For quantity surveyors working in or for the public sector, however, it was generally a busy time with the added ingredient of high inflation. During the 1950s and 1960s, retail price inflation had averaged 3.5 per cent per annum; in the 1970s, it was rarely below ten per cent and peaked at 26 per cent in 1975. Construction price inflation was higher still.

Fixed price building contracts, particularly in the public sector, became fluctuating price contracts. That is, the client took the responsibility for increases in the cost of labour and materials during the course of a contract. This could be done by monitoring and adjusting actual costs but was more commonly done with the use of price adjustment formulae.[2] This removed at least some of the contractors' risks, particularly on long-term projects but also created opportunities for manipulating payments.

The role of the quantity surveyor as the accountant of the construction industry was probably at its peak in the 1970s. Cost limits, cost planning, cost analysis and the administration of fluctuating price contracts, on top of the preparation of full bills of quantities in accordance with the Standard Method of Measurement, were all complicated and labour intensive activities. The systems were devised by quantity surveyors in public service and largely administered by quantity surveyors in private practice.

The 1970s saw the country move to decimal currency, and the UK construction industry, but not the property industry, move from the imperial to the metric system of measurement. There were also experimental moves to investigate operational bills, bills of quantities that attempted to describe how the project could be built and giving the locations, as well as the quantities of work items. And there was ongoing work on the computerisation of bills of quantities. It was an interesting time to be a quantity surveyor.

In 1972, the Property Services Agency (PSA) was formed to act as the central budget holder for all building works for government. It was effectively the government client and had great influence on the award of work and the ways in which it would be carried out. But by the 1980s, the PSA was under threat from government reforms and it had gone by 1992.

The 1980s brought major changes to the construction industry including the construction professions. Some of these had been coming for a while and their impact had brought about permanent changes in practices and relationships. One of the most far reaching stemmed from the competition authorities decreeing that mandatory fee scales were anti-competitive. The debate about the professions had started in the late 1960s, quantity surveyors' fees were referred to the Prices and Incomes Board in 1969, but it was not until 1983 that fixed fee scales were finally abandoned. This did not have a dramatic effect immediately, at least not in London, largely because the market was good and demand for quantity surveying services was high but, through the decade, fee bidding and price competition became more common.

Also in the 1980s, the RICS permitted members and practices to advertise and practices to adopt company structures other than partnerships. It still, however, required all partners and directors of 'chartered quantity surveyors' to be RICS qualified. Like most firms, L&E and DB&E both described themselves as chartered quantity surveyors.

The late 1970s and early 1980s also saw new forms of development, new developers and new ways of working. These were particularly important because of the increasing importance of private sector development and the relative decline in public sector construction investment. One of the early innovations was 'air rights' development, over railway tracks, and the first of these was at Victoria Station, designed by Elsom Pack & Roberts (EPR).

Three other innovative schemes are indicative of what was possible: the Broadgate development on the site of Broad Street Station and Stockley Park in West London, both involving the developer, Stuart Lipton; and Canary Wharf, initiated by an American developer, G Ware Travelstead, then taken over by the Canadian developers, Olympia & Yorke. These three schemes brought new models of workspaces and new ways of thinking about the development and the construction process. Neither DB&E nor L&E was initially involved with these developers or these ways of working at this stage. Lipton's main quantity surveyor at the time was VJ Mendoza & Partners, a small firm, no longer in existence.[3] Mendoza worked closely with mechanical and electrical quantity surveyors, Mott Green & Wall (MGW) who were to become part of Davis Langdon in the 1990s. DB&E and, subsequently, DL&E were involved in later stages of Stockley Park.

Although the construction industry, contractors and consultants, was determinedly private sector, there were a number of public sector agencies that were important to the industry.[4] They included the National Building Agency (NBA), established in 1964, largely to advise on the housing programme;

the Construction Committees of the National Economic Development Council (NEDC), created by the Wilson government to provide a forum for government, industry and the unions; and the Building Research Establishment (BRE), dating back to the 1920s and the government's advisor on construction related matters. NBA was privatised in the early 1980s and produced a number of specialised consultancies, the successors of which still exist. The NEDC was sidelined and eventually disbanded in the early 1990s. The PSA and BRE were progressively detached from government during the 1980s and prepared for privatisation.

Langdon & Every

In 1970, L&E had eight UK partners, all based in London, in Aldwych House: Porter, the senior partner, Giles Every, Brearley, Holmes, Maclean, Berryman, Driscoll and McLeod. Porter and Holmes retired in 1973 and 1978, respectively, and Every replaced Porter as senior partner in 1973 at the age of 42.[5] Holmes and McLeod had been partners in the Far East practice and Maclean and Driscoll had been partners in the Middle East. There was something of a tradition of overseas partners coming back to the UK and becoming UK partners. There were eight regional offices: in Chester, Edinburgh, Harlow, Liverpool, Manchester, Plymouth, Portsmouth and Southampton. Total staff in the UK was over 300, including partners.

Well-known office building projects undertaken by L&E in London in the 1970s, included Numbers 4 and 8 Bishopsgate, designed by Gollins Melvin Ward (GMW) for Banque Belge and Baring Brothers, respectively, developments of GMW's Commercial Union and P&O buildings, built in the 1960s (also with L&E as quantity surveyors); and the Kings Reach development on the South Bank of the Thames, designed by Richard Seifert & Partners. The redevelopment of Euston Station, designed by Siefert with L&E as quantity surveyors, also included a series of office towers. L&E also did other projects for the London Midland Region of British Rail.

Also in London, there were town centre developments at Ealing and Lewisham, for Grosvenor Estates; work for London University; schools and housing projects for the Greater London Council; film and television studio projects; and work on historic buildings with Seely and Paget, who L&E had worked with since the 1920s. Outside London, there were building projects for the Army and the Navy, major hospital projects, university buildings, including Heriot Watt University in Edinburgh, racecourse grandstands, including Goodwood, designed by HV Lobb with Sir Philip Dowson, and schools and housing projects.

By this time, L&E were heavily involved in major power, industrial and process engineering projects. Work on Sizewell B power station started in the 1970s and continued for 20 years. Major North Sea oil finds in the late 1960s led to a major involvement by L&E in petrochemical projects through the 1970s, including accommodation and service modules for oil rigs, building on the knowledge and expertise gained on power station and industrial projects.

The UK offices were also involved in international projects. A certain amount of Middle East work was done in the UK, and there was also work for Middle East clients in the UK. Colin Brearley, who was the partner mainly involved with GMW, was asked to undertake an advisory role on their new BOAC (British Overseas Airways Corporation) terminal at JFK Airport in New York. And Mike McLeod was involved in a series of projects in Nigeria in association with a local firm of quantity surveyors. This was in the mid-1970s when Nigeria was newly 'oil rich'; projects included radio stations and schools and an office building in Lagos.

Offices for Banque Belge and Baring Brothers in Bishopsgate, GMW.

In the 1980s, prior to the merger with DB&E, Colin Brearley, Ken Maclean and Jim Driscoll retired and three new partners were invited to join the partnership: Alan Willis, Derek Lawrence and Fraser Anderson.[6] Willis had worked for DB&E in the 1960s and in South Africa for five years before joining L&E in the mid-1970s; Lawrence joined about the same time as a personal assistant to Ken Maclean and worked extensively on overseas projects; Anderson had been a partner in the Middle East practice, in Bahrain. All three were around 40 in 1985. In the 1980s, the Chester, Edinburgh and Harlow offices of L&E were closed.

But the major unanticipated change in the partnership in the 1980s was the death in a motor car accident of Giles Every in 1984. He and his wife were

Top: Grandstand at Goodwood, Howard Lobb Partnership with Sir Philip Downson.

Bottom: Heriot Watt University, Reiach & Hall.

both killed instantly driving home from Ascot. Giles had been his father's nominated successor, he became a partner in 1961 and senior partner when John Porter retired. On Giles' death, Ken Maclean was immediately appointed as senior partner and, some time later, Giles' interests in the overseas practices were taken over by the remaining UK partners.

In notes to the staff, Giles Every wrote in March 1982 that the practice "has been far from busy for many months"; but things evidently picked up shortly afterwards. In 1984, Giles noted what the press had described as the government's "attack on the professions" resulting in "firstly, a greater freedom to publicise ourselves and be much more aggressive in seeking work and, secondly, the virtual abandonment of fee scales with an increasing amount of work being subject to competitive tender on fees". He went on to say that "gone, probably for ever are the relative comforts of scale fees with the ability for us to do a really professional job without having to worry overmuch about the cost".

Oil production and wellhead installation, Hoorn Field, Offshore Netherlands. Courtesy Unocal Netherlands Inc..

In Ken Maclean's note in 1985, he talks about the partnership "being at a crossroads" and reports on plans for closer integration with Langdon Every & Seah in South-East Asia; he goes on to say "at home, the pace of change quickens and we need to be sure that we maintain our position in this changing scene". In 1986, he again comments on "the considerable pressure on fees" and says that "it is clear that we will have to increase our efforts to provide an effective and economical service to our clients". Shortly after this, of course, Maclean met Bill Fussell of DB&E to initiate the merger discussions.

Despite all these changes, the firm was still busy working for both old and new clients. One of the newer clients was Bupa the private healthcare provider, where the firm acted as client advisor and, effectively, project manager as well as quantity surveyor. They also worked on healthcare buildings for the Nuffield Trust. There were projects with the Bank of England, with Wilson Mason & Partners as architects. They worked on GMW's Commercial Union building after it had been damaged by an IRA bomb and, just as that work was finishing, it was hit by another bomb.

Prestige office building projects continued with No. 4 The Strand, west of Charing Cross Station, designed by Casson Conder & Partners. And, also with Casson Conder there was an early scheme for the New Parliamentary building on Bridge Street, Westminster and a new opera house at the Royal College of Music in Kensington. And work continued at Ascot racecourse where L&E had had an office for decades.

Outside London, there was a wide variety of projects, but particularly in industrial engineering and petrochemicals, centred on the Manchester office but with staff all over the country. This kind of work was a major, but largely unrealised, attraction in the merger discussions at the end of the decade.

Langdon & Every had a small but dedicated IT department in the 1980s and had bespoke software applications for a number of major projects, including power stations (Hinkley C and Sizewell B) and Ascot. LES in Hong Kong had developed quantity surveying software called ATLES, that was adopted by DLE after the two firms merged.

Left: Alan Berryman

Right: From left to right, Derek Lawrence, Mike McLeod, Alan Willis.

Davis Belfield & Everest

DB&E in the 1970s was making the transition from the founder partners to the next generation, one that L&E had already made. Davis, Everest, Parrinder and Mill all retired between 1971 and 1978 and became consultants, as set out in the partnership arrangements devised by Davis and Geoff Trickey in the late 1960s.[7] At the end of the 1970s, therefore, there were seven partners: Fussell, Milborne, Nick Davis, Trickey, Malby, Venning and Morrell; two in their 50s, three in their 40s, one, Davis, in his 30s and the last, Morrell, in his 20s.

The origins of the new partners varied. Fussell, who joined as a partner, was apparently recommended by the RICS; Milborne was an in-house promotion, he had been with the firm for 12 years; and Davis was, of course, Owen Davis' son. Trickey, Malby and Venning were all born in 1935. Trickey was with the firm in the early 1960s, left to join the National Building Agency and was invited back as a partner two years later. Malby was another in-house promotion, he had been with the firm for nine years (after ten years with EC Harris & Partners) and was something of a protégé of Everest's; and Venning was an old colleague of Malby's recruited to take over responsibility for mechanical and electrical services. Paul Morrell was an in-house promotion, although a very young one, he was only 28 when invited to become a partner. He had been on the point of moving when the partnership was offered at least partly to pre-empt this.

In 1970, the firm moved from Ashley Place, Victoria, where they had been since the end of the Second World War, to Nos. 5, 6 and 7 Golden Square on the edge of Soho. This was an imposing five-storey red brick self-contained office building on the east side of the Square.[8] The ground floor of No. 6 was sub-let to a small and relatively new firm of public relations consultants called Saatchi & Saatchi. [9]

There were 11 branch offices, seven established in the 1940s, 1950s and 1960s, Cambridge, Chester, Gateshead, Leeds, Newport, Norwich and Oxford, and four new, Portsmouth, 1974, Milton Keynes, 1976, Ipswich, 1977 and Glasgow, 1979, with a total staff of around 180 people. All except one of the branch offices was originally established to service local projects won by the firm. The exception was Portsmouth, which was established speculatively and initially fed with work from London. Prior to that, the firm had no offices on the South Coast and felt that they should have.

DB&E's workload in the 1970s was predominantly, but not exclusively, public sector, varied and extensive. The Barbican project was still under construction and the 1970s saw the start of the Arts Centre, the final stage

The DB&E offices at Nos. 5, 6 and 7, Golden Square, London in the 1970s.

of the Barbican development. There was also initial work on the National Theatre, designed by Denys Lasdun & Partners, and the British Library, designed by Colin St John Wilson, both initially on different sites to the ones they ended up on. The firm worked on the Post Office Research Laboratory at Martlesham Heath in Suffolk for the Property Services Agency.

There were also projects for private sector clients, notably the new head office for Willis Faber Dumas in Ipswich, designed by Foster & Partners. And there were major overseas projects in the Middle East, including the King Faisal Hospital in Ryadh, Saudi Arabia, commissioned initially by Vickers Medical and designed by Hospital Design Partnership, and health projects in Iran and Iraq with Yorke Rosenberg Mardall and Llewellyn Davies. Although these were major long-term projects, the firm never took the step of establishing offices outside the UK.

In the 1980s there were three more partners appointed before the merger with Langdon & Every and two retirements. The new partners were Rob Smith, in 1982, who had been the associate in charge of the cost research department; Jon Stanwyck, in 1984, brought in to take over M&E services from Patrick Venning; and Simon Johnson in 1986. The retirements were Milborne and Fussell in 1985 and 1986, respectively. Helping to initiate the merger discussions was one of Fussell's last acts as a partner.[10]

Willis Faber Dumas head office, Ipswich, Foster & Partners.

One of the striking things about the 1980s was the pressure to reduce project delivery times. For an industry that was used to major projects taking decades this was a challenge. The firm were quantity surveyors on Heathrow Terminal 4, for British Airports Authority, designed by Scott Brownrigg & Turner. They were appointed in 1978, work started in 1980 and the project was handed over for fitting out by British Airways in 1985. At the time the £200 million project was the largest management contract in Europe.

Central Square Uxbridge in West London was one of DB&E's first speculative commercial development projects. It was a ten-storey office building with 24,000 square metres gross floor area and the client wanted early completion; the original programme was 14 months to get on site and 24 months construction. In the event, the 14 months was relaxed due to delays in gaining approvals but the contract was delivered only three weeks over the 24 months. The procurement route was an innovative hybrid of traditional and management contracts.

The DB&E partners at the partners' table on the fifth floor of Golden Square in 1983. Left to right, Nick Davis, Dick Milborne, Bill Fussell, Patrick Venning, Clyde Malby, Geoff Trickey, Paul Morrell and Rob Smith.

Other projects in the 1980s included a new headquarters building for British Nuclear Fuels Ltd in Warrington, designed by Duffy Eley Giffone & Worthington (DEGW); the Clore Gallery at Tate Britain for the Turner Collection, and Tate in the North in Liverpool Docks, both designed by James Stirling & Michael Wilford.

The 1980s also saw the introduction of in-house computing. Although computerised bills of quantities had been around since the 1960s, there were no computers in DB&E offices until the early 1980s. The first machine was a large blue cupboard-sized Data General mini-computer with a small number of terminals, installed primarily to run the accounts system. Later, a mini-computer also ran the CATO (Computer Aided Taking Off) measurement system.

Terminals for surveyors were un-networked Commodore PETs with 32k of memory and 5¼ inch floppy disks that held 343k of data. By the mid-1980s there were 30 terminals in London and a few in most branch offices. Software was 'standard' spreadsheet and word processing programs and 'bespoke' programs produced in-house by the cost research department for surveying tasks such as developers' budgets, initial estimates and cash flow forecasts. Simon Johnson, discussing the future of new technologies in a *DB&E News* of 1986, predicted the era of "24 hour a day links with the office" and was wise enough to question whether this would be a good thing. At that time, the technology was available but expensive and not particularly user-friendly. Johnson went on to comment "whether the computer will ever replace the paper and pen completely is questionable but there can be little doubt that the computer will be as common as the calculator, the only question is how long will that take?" The answer was ten years.

Terminal 4 under construction,
Scott, Brownrigg & Turner.

Commentary

The diagram below shows the progression of partners in both firms through the 1970s and 1980s to their merger in 1988. The DB&E pattern is uncannily smooth, a tribute to the early partners' careful succession planning. The L&E pattern is more untidy, partly due to the partners' habit of taking on 'mature' partners (who had been partners in overseas practices) but also because of the tragic and sudden death of Giles Every in 1984 at the age of 53. Under L&E's partnership rules, he would have been a partner and senior partner for a further 12 years. Relative to the firms' sizes, however, L&E's five partners broadly corresponded with DB&E's eight.

	1970		1975		1980		1985	
Langdon & Every (1955-1988)								
JH Porter								
G Every								
AW Berryman								
CC Brearley								
CR Holmes								
KA Maclean								
JA Driscoll								
MA McLeod								
AC Willis								
DR Lawrence								
JF Anderson								
Davis Belfield & Everest (1944-1988)								
OA Davis								
RL Everest								
SF Mill								
ER Parrinder								
WFJ Fussell								
RAE Milborne								
NA Davis								
GG Trickey								
CC Malby								
PC Venning								
PD Morrell								
RJ Smith								
JA Stanwyck								
SR Johnson								

Diagram showing the partners in L&E and DB&E from 1970 to 1988 (continued from page 54).

It is worth noting, although it was not unusual for the industry or the profession, that neither firm had a female partner. Like most of the rest of the construction industry, quantity surveyors were very slow in attracting, or allowing, women into the highest tiers of the profession. It was to be more than ten years before the first female partner was appointed, and that would be via merger.

Fee competition in the public sector finally brought to an end the situation whereby quantity surveyors could be appointed on the recommendation of architects. By the end of the 1980s, virtually every commission of any size was the subject of fee competition. The situation varied in the private sector; some clients adopted fee bidding but many continued with direct appointments but expected competitive fees.

As suggested in the title of this chapter, the two decades but, particularly, the 1980s saw the end of what has been called the post-war consensus. For the next 20 years a market oriented approach replaced the directed economy that had largely prevailed since 1945. Whatever L&E and DB&E had done, they would have had to adapt to the new conditions that appear after the early 1990s recession ended.

1   This graph can be compared to those on page 38 (1955 to 1970) and page 118 (1988 to 2005). All three are compiled on the same basis and drawn to the same scale.
2   Cyril Sweett devised standard formulae for building price fluctuation for the National Economic Development Council in the late 1960s.
3   VJ Mendoza & Partners was bought by the Bucknall Group in 1995.
4   As an aside, nationalisation had been discussed in the mid-1970s and an industry organisation, CABIN (Campaign Against Building Industry Nationalisation), had been formed to resist it but the moment passed. It is interesting to contrast the prospect with the attitudes to industry from 1979 onwards.
5   John Porter died in 1982, and Dick Holmes in 2006.
6   Ken Maclean died in 2003, and Colin Brearley in 2008.
7   Owen Davis died in 1992, Bobbie Everest in 1977 and John Parrinder in 1980.
8   The building was demolished and rebuilt in the 1990s after the firm moved to Princes House. Clyde Malby salvaged the front door and had it installed at his home in South London.
9   Latterly, the same space was sub-let to Broadway Malyan, architects and planners.
10   Fussell died in 1994, aged 68, and Milborne died in 2008, aged 83.

Chapter Five

Working Nationally

Although every British firm of quantity surveyors of any size now has a network of offices in the UK this was not always the case. Before the Second World War, multi-office firms were extremely unusual. After the war branch offices were established to service major projects or clients; alternatively, they were acquired through the merger or acquisition of another firm. Thereafter, they were maintained if a suitable individual emerged and sufficient workload existed. The process tended to be rather haphazard.

More recently, development of a national network has been a more strategic exercise with the location, size and composition of offices being carefully planned. Davis Langdon has some 20 offices in the UK, including London but excluding site offices. The map below shows the location of permanent offices in 2008.

Davis Langdon UK Offices, 2008.

The Langdon & Every Provincial Offices

In the mid-1930s Tom Every noted that only one major firm, Gleeds, had more than one office, in Bristol, opened in the 1920s. Against the conventional practice of the time, however, Horace W Langdon & Every (HWL&E) was determined to open offices outside London in the 1930s, not least because they had two bright young men, John Winship and Edward Thornton Firkin, to head them. A Southampton office was opened in 1935 with Winship in charge. He became a partner, three or four years later, but only having an interest in the newly formed Langdon Every & Winship (LE&W).[1] Winship had been an articled pupil with Langdon and they were close personally (his son was Langdon's godson). The initial rationale for Southampton was the anticipated development of the dockyards; before the war, the firm also worked on a Spitfire fighter plane factory at Woolston.

Shortly after, in 1938, the firm was encouraged to set up in the North-West of England by Sir Thomas White, Mayor of Liverpool and Chairman of Bent's Brewery.[2] For some reason, White did not want the firm to come to Liverpool so an office was opened in Hanley, Stoke on Trent where Forshaw & Greaves, main architects to the brewery, were based and for many years HWL&E undertook all Bent's work in the Potteries. Thornton Firkin was put in charge and, like the Southampton venture, he became local partner of Langdon Every & Firkin (LE&F) two years later, again, only having an interest in that firm. At around the same time, an office was opened in Lincoln.

As war became inevitable, the firm was increasingly busy on government contracts, including military camps and airfields for the RAF, and the advantages of having provincial offices became evident.[3] Government departments in London liked to give work to the London firms they knew and trusted. Construction work was necessarily all over the country and there were logistical problems for the London firms to get to the more remote locations and pressure from local (usually smaller) firms to be awarded work in their locale. HWL&E's provincial offices provided the ideal of a local service from a London firm.

All the work on Salisbury Plain for the War Department was given to LE&W and aerodromes in Lincolnshire went to LE&F. Horace Langdon, himself, spent a year at Bulford Camp on Salisbury Plain. Subsequently an office was opened in Salisbury from 1941 to 1944. A branch of LE&W was opened in Plymouth to undertake work in the South-West and they were appointed four aerodromes in Exeter, Portreath, Penanport and Prudanwork Downs. In 1943 and 1944, senior staff, including Ivan

Lankester, later manager in London, spent time at Anthorn in Cumberland on a major Admiralty Air Field.

In 1944, LE&W opened an office in Fareham in Hampshire and four years later this moved to Portsmouth, to Coronation House, where it remained for 50 years. In 1988, at the time of their merger with DB&E, L&E had offices in Southampton, Plymouth and Portsmouth and the first two are still there as the longest established Davis Langdon provincial offices.

Britain emerged from the Second World War battered and impoverished but not unplanned. An enormous amount of effort was expended during the war, starting as early as 1942, to prepare government and the British people for the post-war era and included buildings and works across the country.[4] The drivers of the post-war building boom and the geographical expansion of professional firms were, initially, repairs and reconstruction; followed by housing and public works, schools and industrial buildings; and, subsequently, hospitals and the expansion of the existing and the new universities and the new towns.

The Simon Report anticipated post-war problems in the construction sector, particularly resource shortages, and measures were put in place to address the main issues and to plan for post-war construction.[5] Building licences for private work continued until 1954 although, over time, it became increasingly easier to obtain them. There were shortages of key materials, including steel and bricks, and there were studies to address and circumvent these. Incentives, registration schemes and training meant that the construction labour force more than doubled in the first decade after the war.

There was also thought given to alternative procurement processes and technologies although it took time for there to be real changes in methods. Immediately after the war, cost-plus was commonly used (as it had been during the war), particularly for repair and maintenance work. Negotiated contracts were also used but not for local authority work. In the 1950s, Model Standing Orders confirmed the general rule of public open tendering.[6] Like most quantity surveying firms, L&E and DB&E had been engaged during the war on mainly government projects and this continued in the immediate post-war period. Quantity surveyors and quantity surveying were an integral part of the construction process, particularly for public works.

In 1946, Thornton-Firkin gave up his partnership in LE&F and set up his own practice which continues today. Around the same time, the Chairman of Bent's Bewery changed and the new Chairman preferred to see the firm in Liverpool. An office was opened in Liverpool although the Stoke office also remained for a few years (both were in existence in 1949). The firm's name reverted to Horace W Langdon & Every, and the first big job in Liverpool was an extension to Bent's brewery itself. R Allen was recruited as manager and became a local partner in 1956.

In the 1950s and 1960s there were housing, school and other, mainly public, projects and major developments at the Royal Liverpool and Fazakerley hospitals. In the late 1960s, the office became involved in process plant work at the British Industrial Plastics (BIP) factory at Whiston and then work on petrochemical and associated civil engineering work at Ellesmere Port. The office continued to develop through the 1970s and 1980s maintaining their involvement in building work and civil and industrial engineering in and around Liverpool. They also worked overseas, in Europe, on industrial engineering projects.

Winship died suddenly in 1951, aged only 38 and, shortly after, the management of the Southampton office was taken over by Reg Brooks and, again, the firm's title reverted to Horace W Langdon & Every.[7] By the 1950s, the firm was working on a range of building types. Alan Berryman, who was there in the early 1950s, recalls offices, schools, garages and cinemas. Frank Angell became the local partner in Southampton when he retired from Singapore in the late 1950s and Brooks moved to London to become a full partner.

Pharmaceutical facility at Terlings Park, Harlow for Merck Sharp & Dohme Limited. Courtesy Kyle Stewart.

In 1953, HWL&E opened an office in Harlow New Town. The firm worked on a range of housing, industrial and public building projects, including the town centre, and acted as general advisors on construction related matters. Colin Brearley joined a study visit to Canada to look at prefabricated timber housing; a small scheme was actually built in Harlow using a Canadian system and Canadian labour but it was not pursued. The Harlow office operated for over 30 years, until 1984.

The first nuclear power station, Calder Hall in Cumbria, was commissioned in 1956 although construction work had commenced in the 1940s. L&E were appointed by the Central Electricity Generating Board (CEGB), later the UK Atomic Energy Authority (UKAEA), to work on the nuclear power station programme and the firm provided full quantity surveying services on major projects at Sellafield in Cumbria (adjacent to Calder Hall), Winfreth in Dorset and Dounray in the North of Scotland. Work on power stations, including Fawley in Hampshire, was to continue for more than 30 years; the firm's last power station project was Sizewell B on the Suffolk coast, finishing in 1995.

In the early 1960s, site office staff at Dounray were transferred to an ICI pharmaceuticals plant at Macclesfield, the firm's introduction to industrial engineering work and, in 1962, the decision was taken to open an office in Manchester to service a number of mainly engineering projects. In the 1970s, L&E became involved in North Sea Oil exploration and extraction with Giles Every as the partner in charge. Don Parkinson, who had joined the firm in 1959 and become a specialist in process work, became manager then local partner in Manchester in 1973. With power, process and petrochemical work, L&E had people all over the country, in Middlesborough, Glasgow, Scunthorpe and Hull, in project and client offices, all managed from Manchester. There was also a permanent office in Aberdeen in the 1970s and 1980s. The petrochemical speciality in Manchester came into its own with the 1980s link-up between the UK and Far East practices, L&E Cost Engineering (LECE) for work with Shell in Brunei.

Left: Royal Liverpool Hospital,
Holford Associates.
Right: Hohen Bridge, Southampton

Fawley Power Station, Hampshire.

The Davis Belfield & Everest Provincial Offices

Davis and Belfield (D&B) did not open any regional offices before the war, they were too young and small a practice and too busy on other things, but they very quickly did, as Davis Belfield & Everest (DB&E), immediately afterwards. Like most quantity surveyors, D&B had worked on government projects during the war, army camps, airfields and the like, all over the country, as had Bobbie Everest, before he joined the partnership in 1944. DB&E were appointed in 1946 to work on a factory in South Wales for the Brynmawr Rubber Company, designed by Architects Co-Partnership with Ove Arup & Partners as engineers. This was one of the largest building projects in Europe after the war; an example of government-led industrial policy; a famous work of architecture; and the largest job DB&E had undertaken at the time. Bill Barnes, who had joined the firm after war service in 1945, moved to Newport the following year to take charge of the project and open an office.

The Brynmawr factory was developed by the government and sold to Dunlop in 1952 but it was never a financial success and was eventually closed down in 1982. Its design brought it a Grade II listing but feasible alternative uses acceptable to all parties were never found and, amid controversy, it was delisted in 1996 and demolished in 1999.

Newport office grew rapidly from the 1950s onwards, mainly on the back of public work, housing, schools, hospitals and industrial projects, for central and local government. In the 1960s, they worked on a headquarters building for the South Wales Electricity Board, designed by Gollins Melvin Ward. Doug Emptage took over the office in 1980.

The Norwich office of DB&E was also established in 1946 to service aerodrome maintenance and reconstruction contracts and, shortly after, a series of rural housing schemes designed by Peter Bicknell. The first manager was a man called Boedeker and, after he emigrated to South Africa in 1948, John Cully took over, became a local partner in 1954 and ran the Norwich office for 20 years. He was succeeded by Bob Lamont who had worked in DB&E Cambridge and then went off to spend ten years in East Africa. Norwich always had a range of interesting projects, including restoration work on Ely Cathedral; other religious buildings; warehouses and industrial buildings for the likes of WH Smith and Colmans; and work for Norwich Union Insurance Company, Norwich City Football Club and the University of East Anglia.

Work in East Anglia in general, and Cambridge in particular, grew and a 21 year old Victor Bugg was sent from Norwich to open an office in 1958. The Cambridge office expanded rapidly in the 1960s and Bugg became a partner in 1964 and established himself and the practice in Cambridge, working extensively in the Colleges as well as on shopping centres, office blocks, churches, hospitals and industrial buildings. As a result of the university connection, DB&E Cambridge joined a consortium of educationalists and building professionals and became involved in a range of educational building projects around the world.

The Brynmawr Rubber Company Factory, Architects Co-Partnership.

The firm had undertaken a number of projects in Ipswich and in Suffolk, since the 1960s, including the Civic Centre, designed by Vine & Vine and, in the early 1970s, the Post Office Research Laboratory at Martlesham Heath, designed by government architects at the Property Services Agency, and the Willis Faber Dumas headquarters, designed by Foster & Partners. In 1977, an office in Ipswich was established as a satellite office of London, working on both local and London projects, including work on Debenhams stores.

In 1956, following appointments for a series of projects in Yorkshire, an office was opened in Leeds. The manager, later partner, was Charles Wheeler, who had joined Owen Davis in 1938, as an office boy on £1 per week, and worked with D&B before going off to war service in 1942. He rejoined the firm, then DB&E, in 1947 and moved to Berkshire to handle its work on the Atomic Weapons Research Establishment at Aldermaston (incidentally, the firm's first multi-million pound project). The Leeds office worked on

Top: The University of East Anglia,
Denys Lasdun & Partners.
Bottom: Post Office Research Centre,
Martlesham Heath, Property Services Agency.

new hospital buildings in Leeds, Whitby, Scarborough and Hull and on schools, Sheffield University, housing schemes and industrial buildings and the International Wool Secretariat building at Ilkley, designed by Chippindale & Edmondson.

An office in Gateshead was opened to support an old client of the firm, the Chief Architect from the Isle of Ely Council, who had been appointed as Chief Architect in Gateshead, and Robert Robinson moved from Norwich to manage it in 1959; he became a local partner in 1963. The Gateshead office worked on factories, schools and housing and on Washington New Town. Two associates in Gateshead, Peter Millidge and Tony Brennan, eventually took over the management of the Gateshead and Leeds offices, became partners and the two offices ran as a single business unit in the 1980s.

An office in Oxford was opened in 1960 with HS Woods as manager. Woods was in charge of work at Aldermaston (following Charles Wheeler) and an Atomic Energy Commission project at Culham and these formed the basis of the new office's workload. The Oxford office worked on College buildings at the University, including a dining hall at St Anthony's College, designed by Howell Killick Partridge & Amis; major hospital projects, notably the John Radcliffe Hospital with Yorke Rosenberg Mardall (YRM), and projects for the Oxford University Press. In the 1960s, there was also a DB&E office in Belfast working on hospital projects, including Londonderry Hospital, designed by YRM and Belfast School of Dentistry, designed by Cardin, Burden & Howitt.

In April 1967, Andrew Thomson moved from the London office to open an office in Chester to handle the new West Cheshire General District Hospital, designed by the Architects Fellowship with Arup as engineers. They also worked on other London projects in the North-West, including a major office building in Manchester, but quickly were generating their own work. Chester office was always keen on doing different things and in 1971 were involved in producing a European section of *Spon's Architects' and Builders' Price Book*. At around the same time they worked with James Stirling and Michael Wilford on the initial cost planning and estimating for the Staatsgalerie in Stuttgart.

In the 1970s, Chester office had two young associates, John Molloy and Tim Carter, both of whom were to become partners. Molloy went on to develop business in the UK and the Middle East in petrochemical and process engineering and Tim Carter took the firm's first steps into the new discipline of project management. Carter's first major appointment was on a Bank of America project in South London.

An office in Portsmouth was opened by DB&E in 1974 by Brian Bartholomew, a young associate from the London office. Much of this office's work was on department stores for Debenhams and C&A and business park and marina developments at Solent for Arlington Securities. An office in Milton Keynes was opened in 1976 to service the firm's work on the New Town, housing, industrial and social buildings. Mike Sharman moved from London to open the office and became a local partner in the 1980s.

An office in Scotland, in Glasgow, was required to work on the Burrell Collection project, won as a result of a major design competition, by Barry Gasson, a lecturer at Cambridge University, and two colleagues. Gasson was based in Cambridge and it was the Cambridge office, and particularly Victor Bugg, the local partner, that supported him and his colleagues in the competition. The job was won in 1972 but work did not start till 1978. The Glasgow office was opened in 1979 by Mike Riddell. Unusually, Bugg had a financial interest in the Glasgow office.

The Burrell Museum was the result of a bequest by Sir William Burrell, a Glasgow shipowner, who had left his substantial and eclectic collection of art and artefacts to the City and people of Glasgow. The conditions of the bequest were difficult to satisfy and it took time and negotiation to agree on a site in the suburbs of Glasgow. The project was complex and DB&E effectively provided project management as well as QS services in its latter stages.

Staatsgalerie, Stuttgart, interior,
James Stirling & Michael Wilford.

Interestingly, at the same time as Cambridge architects were working on a prestigious project in Glasgow, Glasgow architects, Gillespie, Kidd and Coia, were working on Robinson College, Cambridge University and both projects had DB&E Cambridge as their quantity surveyors. Robinson College, Cambridge's newest college was founded after Sir David Robinson gave the university £17 million. Both the Burrell and Robinson College were award-winning designs.

An office in Bristol was opened in 1982 that worked on a range of projects, including an office building for Sun Alliance and London Assurance Co Ltd. It was managed by John Hollier, who became a partner a few years later. In the late 1980s, a separate Bristol office was established to accommodate DB&E Computer Systems, headed by Mark Elwell, who had been an IT consultant to the firm in its first tentative steps into computerising the business, not just the production of bills of quantities. Elwell then joined and was, briefly, a partner in DB&E. David Wood, a long-standing associate, was also based in the Computer Systems office at this stage, working on quantity surveying related computer applications: Cashflow, Developers' Budgets and Cost Estimating.

In 1987/1988, the last full financial year before the merger with L&E, DB&E had a national turnover of £12.4 million of which around £6 million was accounted for by 11 non-London offices. The biggest offices were Portsmouth, Chester and Cambridge, all with turnovers of more than £1 million. Almost three decades years earlier, in 1960, there were four DB&E non-London offices with a combined turnover of just less than £100,000 representing 36 per cent of a total national turnover of £274, 000. Gross profit was 29 per cent in 1960 and 25 per cent in 1988 and, overall, the profitability of London and non-London offices was similar (although there were dramatic differences between individual non-London offices in particular years). Comparable non-London data is not available for L&E as it effectively operated as a single national practice.

Davis Langdon and Regionalisation

The 1980s saw steady growth in construction demand, particularly from private sector developers but it was also the beginning of a new kind of construction, largely led by the private sector, clients and contractors. For quantity surveyors there were major changes: mandatory fee scales were abandoned, advertising was permitted, alternative procurement procedures were introduced and new corporate structures explored. For firms outside London, the first of these had a particular impact: fees were already under pressure and that pressure was more difficult to resist in the provinces. And that led to other changes, including more aggressive marketing and different service offerings.

Top: Civic Offices for the Borough of Milton Keynes, Faulkner-Brown Hendy Watkinson & Stonor.
Centre left: International Wool Secretariat, Ilkley, Chippendale & Edmondson.
Centre right: Burrell Museum and Art Gallery, Glasgow, Barry Gasson.
Bottom: Robinson College, Cambridge, Gillespie Kidd & Coia in association with Yorke Rosenberg Mardall.

Some of the DB&E and L&E provincial offices had developed particular specialisms: petrochemical, overseas work and project management in DB&E Chester; educational projects in DB&E Cambridge; petrochemical and process engineering in L&E Manchester; and civil engineering in L&E Liverpool. But most non-London offices were still general practices providing traditional quantity surveying services on building projects, largely in their local areas. That is, they were largely undifferentiated from their competitors and, once fee competition became common, it was impossible not to join in.

Some non-London offices were also becoming larger and were moving beyond the first generation of local partners. Both the DB&E and L&E models of local partners and managers were beginning to become difficult to sustain. The L&E model included bonuses but no equity participation; the DB&E model included equity and profit participation but only in the local partners' own offices. Both models worked best when offices were relatively new or relatively small but neither provided real career prospects for any but the resident partner or partners. While the *status quo* was, more or less, acceptable to the older members of the various offices, it was not particularly attractive to younger recruits who were less amenable to the barriers against career progression. A particular quirk of the DB&E structure was that provincial offices might well compete with each other, to the surprise of their clients and the dismay of some, but only some, partners.

The merger in 1988 came at the right time for both London and non-London partners, managers and staff. Unintentionally, perhaps, it provided the beginnings of a solution to some of the emerging structural problems and the merger itself provided a fillip to internal and external relationships. Suddenly two successful but rather traditional firms of quantity surveyors presented unforeseen opportunities. The provincial partners and managers were informed of the merger proposal in late 1987 and all offices had a screening of the merger video in March 1988, simultaneously with the London staff presentation at the Institute of Directors. The partners and managers were enthused but, more importantly, the staff, with very few exceptions, saw it as positive, bold and full of opportunities. In the event, for a number of reasons (including a major recession), it took a few years before real progress could be achieved.

At the time of the merger, L&E had five provincial offices and DB&E had 12; L&E had four local salaried partners and one local manager and DB&E had 16 local partners. The table opposite lists the locations of the offices.

Surprisingly, the two firms only overlapped in one provincial city, Portsmouth, although there were a small number of 'near misses', including, for example,

Davis Belfield & Everest		Langdon & Every
Bristol	Leeds	Liverpool
Cambridge	Milton Keynes	Manchester
Chester	Newport	Portsmouth
Gateshead	Norwich	Plymouth
Glasgow	Oxford	Southampton
Ipswich	Portsmouth	

Chester (DB&E) and Liverpool (L&E): only a few miles apart and serving, broadly similar markets.

The early days saw relatively little change for most of the staff in non-London offices. Partners and managers were involved in the organisation and implementation of new structures. A number of former L&E local partners and managers became equity and profit sharing partners in the new firm and there were some new DB&E partners. New non-London partners adopted the DB&E model of participation only in their own offices. In any case, in what seemed like no time at all, the whole firm was coping with the worst recession the construction industry had experienced since the Second World War. The focus of partners and staff was on survival rather than change. It was not until the early 1990s that thoughts returned to new organisational models and arrangements.

Pressures for regionalisation started in the difficult years in the early 1990s. There was concern about the long-term viability of small (less than 20 people) and single partner offices. At the same time, there was a desire to move towards a national practice rather than a London dominated ownership structure. This began, unsurprisingly, with some administrative and financial tidying up. Historically, administrative and financial and technical and information resources were centralised in London; only London could justify the equivalent of a full time company secretary and support staff, a comprehensive technical library with dedicated staff and specialist departments, for example, for cost planning or mechanical and electrical services. Part of the move towards all partners participating in a national practice was for everyone to contribute to these central services.

Until the 1990s, growth in the regions was essentially organic with offices succeeding largely because they grew a local business with local clients. From the early 1990s, steps were taken to supplement local resources by strategic mergers and acquisitions: the merger with Clarence Smart & Partners in Peterborough provided an office in another major town in the East Anglia Region; the merger with Leighton & Wright in 1999 provided management

Table showing DB&E and L&E provincial offices in 1988.

support to South Wales; the merger with Poole Stokes & Wood the same year increased the staff and management resources of the North-West region; and the merger with Stockings & Clark in 2001 brought expertise in food processing plants; more recently, the merger with Mackenzies in 2007 has transformed the Scottish offices into a major region. Importantly, all of these moves involved discussion and agreement at management board as well as local levels, they were genuinely national initiatives.

A Birmingham office was acquired through the merger with Poole Stokes & Wood in 1999. There had previously been attempts to establish a presence in Birmingham as it was seen as a gap in the national network but these had been unsuccessful. In 2003, when the London office was moving from Princes House to MidCity Place, the opportunity was taken to move the majority of the central business services staff to Birmingham. This, combined with the technical staff there, justified a bigger office and a better presence and simultaneously reduced the firm's overheads. Most of Davis Langdon's Financial, Human Resources and IT staff are now based in Birmingham.

The main points in favour of a single national practice were that it would encourage working together and exchanging contacts and work among offices; the main points against were that it would 'featherbed' underperforming offices and tend to conceal any underperformance. The arrangement that was thrashed out in the early 1990s involved all partners contributing to, and sharing in, a national profit pool while, at the same time, the provincial partners agreed to buy out the future expectations of the London partners and contribute to central services. Needless to say, it is easier to write that than it was in practice to agree the numbers. In simple terms, all offices contributed, initially, 20 per cent of their profits to a national pool and drew from that pool in proportion to their contribution to profit. The remainder of their income came from their own office profit. This financial model was tweaked over time but remained essentially unchanged until the "One Firm One Future" initiative in 2008.

The non-London partners also agreed to buy out the London partners' interest in their offices over a ten year period from future earnings. In practice, the London partners were paid immediately from a loan taken out with the firm's bankers and the provincial partners paid off the loan in proportion to their office profits.

East Anglia was the first 'region' to emerge. Cambridge, Norwich and Ipswich had close historic ties and were used to working together. Ipswich became a branch office in 1988, without an equity partner, but never achieved critical mass and was closed in 1998 with the staff moving to Norwich. East Anglia expanded into an Anglia/Midlands region, taking in Milton Keynes, Birmingham and Peterborough, the last two by mergers. Birmingham was a Poole Stokes & Wood office (and one of the rationales for that merger). Peterborough office came with the merger with Clarence Smart & Partners in 1996.

The North-West (Chester, Liverpool and Manchester) and the North-East (Leeds and Gateshead) developed separately and were then combined in a Northern region. Chester office was absorbed into Liverpool and Manchester and the Poole Stokes & Wood merger helped create critical mass in the North-West. Gateshead moved to Newcastle but was eventually closed. Leeds continued and Manchester and Liverpool made up the Northern region.

The Southern region incorporating the offices into South-East and South-West was the most difficult region to create and the process was kick-started by Rob Smith, the London managing partners, first, by being absorbed into a greater 'London and South' region comprising London office and Bristol, Plymouth, Portsmouth, Oxford, Southampton and South Wales. After a few years, the non-London offices were de-merged as the Southern region.

An office was opened in Cardiff in 1990 and Newport and Cardiff ran in parallel for a few years then Newport was closed in 1994. Since 1998, the Cardiff office has been managed by Paul Edwards and Jim Leighton. In recent years the firm has worked on major commercial developments on Cardiff Bay and extensively in the public sector across South Wales.

Three offices have been added in the last decade or so: Maidstone, opened as a satellite of London, Stevenage emerged as a result of the merger with Schumann Smith, and the 2012 Olympics office in Canary Wharf in London Docklands. The Maidstone office was established in 1997 to provide services on an 800 acre site for the developer, Rouse Kent, but has since emerged as an office serving the Thames Gateway and the South-East of England. As with many of the earlier offices, the origins of Maidstone and Canary Wharf are as project office and the latter may well close in 2012 or shortly thereafter; and Stevenage is now being integrated with London.

The Glasgow office struggled after the Burrell project was completed but there was a will in the partnership to maintain an office and build a practice in Scotland. In the mid-1980s, Hugh Fisher who had been with Dansken & Purdie, an old Glasgow firm, in their Liverpool office, was appointed to take over the Glasgow office. Four years later, with the help of the London office, Glasgow was appointed as quantity surveyors on the Museum of Scotland project in Chambers Street, Edinburgh. The project was the result of another design competition won by the London based firm

of Benson & Forsyth. The design was controversial and the Prince of Wales resigned as patron of the museum, echoing his 'carbuncle' criticisms of the National Gallery competition several years earlier. The project, however, kept the Scottish office busy and justified the opening of an Edinburgh office. It finished in 1998 and was a Stirling Prize runner up the following year.

The Scottish Parliament building was yet another competition, this time won by the Catalan architect Enric Miralles, in association with local architects, RMJM, in 1998. Construction commenced in 1999 and the building was officially opened by the Queen in 2004, receiving the Stirling Prize the following year. The building, however, is now at least as famous for its cost overruns as its architecture. Lord Fraser was appointed to undertake an inquiry into the project and his report is critical of most project participants, particularly the civil servants. Davis Langdon received less criticism than some others in the building team but the project was a hard lesson in how the firm should respond to very complex projects.

Sadly, Ian McAndie, the project partner, died in the final year of the project having dedicated the last part of his life to its successful completion. He is appropriately acknowledged towards the end of the introduction to Lord Fraser's report, as follows:

> In my view at relatively early stages a number of decisions were taken which were fundamentally wrong or wholly misleading. It is the consequences of these decisions which have caused the massive increases in costs and delays. Coupled with that the situation was admirably summed up in a curt handwritten note by Mr Ian McAndie, a partner at Davis Langdon & Everest as far back as March 1999: "Nobody tells Enric to think about economy with any seriousness." Little in this Report improves on that early astute observation.

Museum of Scotland, Benson & Forsyth.
Photographer: Keith Hunter/arcaid.co.uk.

In 2004, as a direct result of the Scottish Parliament experience, the firm started work on a formal project review process that eventually became "DLivering Success". The partners decided that doing nothing when projects were running into difficulties was not an option.

In 2004, the year the Fraser Inquiry report was published, Sam Mackenzie, a London partner and native Scot, volunteered to move to Glasgow as resident partner. There was little fee-earning work, staff had been preoccupied with the Parliament building and the inquiry, many had left and those that remained were demoralised. It took a couple of years to restore morale and build up the workload but, by early 2007, the Scottish offices were a viable business. For at least ten years a merger partner had been sought in Scotland, but without success. In February 2007 Mackenzie was introduced to the directors of Mackenzies, one of the larger Scottish QS firms but not one that had been courted previously. The principals of both firms got on well and by July the merger was finalised. In 2008, the firm in Scotland had a total staff of 150 in three offices, Glasgow, Edinburgh and Aberdeen, and a turnover of £11 million.

Scottish Parliament, Enric Miralles Benedetta Tagliabue/RMJM.

Locations	Turnover £000s	Number of Staff	Number of Partners	Origin
Southern England and Wales				
Bristol	3,350	33	4	Opened by DB&E in 1982
Cardiff	5,432	51	4	Originally DB&E in Newport, opened in 1946, Cardiff office opened in 1990
Oxford	3,293	39	3	Opened by DB&E in 1960
Plymouth	1,846	28	3	Opened by L&E during the Second World War
Southampton	6,368	62	9	Opened by L&E in th mid-1930s
Maidstone	2,155	21	2	Originally a satellite of London. opened in 1997
Stevenage	6,104	39	4	Acquired with Schumann Smith in 1999
Olympics	6,593	28	5	Opened by DL in 2007
Anglia Midlands				
Birmingham	4,814	61	5	Acquired with Poole Stokes & Wood 1999
Cambridge	4,000	54	5	Opened by DB&E in 1958
Milton Keynes	7,040	77	8	Opened by DB&E in 1976
Norwich	5,919	63	5	Opened by DB&E in 1946
Peterborough	3,439	46	2	Acquired with Clarence Smart & Partners in 1996
Northern				
Leeds	1,575	46	2	Opened by DB&E in 1956
Liverpool	5,449	69	7	Originally L&E in Stoke-on-Trent, opened in 1938, Liverpool office opened 1946
Manchester	6,586	67	8	Opened by L&E in 1962
Scotland				
Aberdeen	465	11	1	Acquired with Mackenzie & Partners in 2007
Edinburgh	1,657	25	3	Opened by DL in 1995
Glasgow	6382	62	10	Opened by DB&E in 1979
Total	82,485	882	90	

Commentary

It is interesting that the original branch office model adopted by Langdon and Every in the 1930s but abandoned in the 1960s was very similar to the DB&E model used from the 1940s and adopted by Davis Langdon in 1988. It is effectively a 'franchise': the local partner can use the national name but only benefit personally from their own local efforts. In the case of DB&E, the local partner or partners could 'own' up to 70 per cent of their office, the London partners, having the rest. We don't know how the early L&E model operated but we do know that Frank Angell was unhappy with it in the 1960s. Victor Bugg's financial interest in the Glasgow, as well as his home, Cambridge, offices hints at the need to tweak the branch office business model on occasion.

By 1988, the non-London offices were generating about half of the firm's turnover up from a third, 30 years earlier. Clearly, branch offices were useful: they provided geographical spread; they also helped to reduce the firm's cost base as well as contributing to income.

Opposite top: Sage, Gateshead, Foster & Partners.

Opposite centre left: Sophos Headquarters, Abingdon, Bennetts Associates.

Opposite right: Belgrade Theatre, Coventry, Stanton Williams.

Opposite bottom left: Cheshire Oaks Outlet Village, Ellesmere Port, Benoy Ltd.

Right: Table showing key data for the non-London offices in 2008.

The arguments for local offices are mostly about serving local clients; the arguments against are mainly to do with the development of a national practice (and a focus on national clients). Regionalisation was intended to provide weight to the local network and to put the various offices and regions into a national context, provincial offices by their nature have to service a provincial market. Although their origins may have been in major projects, often their future development has relied on servicing local clients and largely local projects of all types and sizes. Another major influence on their development has been the interests and enthusiasms of their senior staff. Yet another has been the development of a service line that was not economical to pursue in London.

There tend to be strong links between local clients and local firms; they used to be virtually exclusive, clients in Liverpool would tend not to use Manchester firms for their work, for example, and *vice versa;* this is not the case today or, at least, not to the same extent, and most large firms of quantity surveyors have national networks but, still today, partners in provincial offices will tend to be local people.

In the past ten years or so, Davis Langdon has developed and consolidated its provincial offices into four regions. The table on the previous page summarises the size and origins of the current non-London offices. As indicated earlier, the firm is moving to a national and sectoral structure but it is likely that regional relationships and loyalties for staff and clients will remain for some time.

The table indicates that, of the current complement, eight offices were opened by Davis Belfield & Everest (DB&E); four by Langdon & Every (L&E); three by Davis Langdon; and four were acquired via mergers with other firms. Over the years, there have been other offices in other locations that have been closed, because the work ran out or because there was no suitable individual to build a business; and, more recently, because they did not fit with the firm's strategy. The total turnover of £82.5 million (£91.5 million with DLC&J) for the non-London offices is around 45 per cent of the firm's total turnover of £190 million and probably around ten times the turnover of the 17 'branch' offices that existed in 1988.

The early 1990s aspiration of every office having at least two partners and 20 staff has almost been achieved. Only Aberdeen, the result of a recent acquisition, does not fit the criteria and was in the process of being closed in late 2008. The target size of offices nowadays is probably closer to 40 staff. It will be interesting to see the future evolution of the non-London offices as the combined impacts of a recession, "One Firm One Future" and the sectoral approach take effect.

1　The "Horace W" prefix in the firm's name was dropped in the provincial offices.

2　Bent's was taken over by Bass Charrington, now Bass plc, in 1967.

3　There were 600 airfields built during the war, all over the country. In 1942, a new airfield was started every three days in East Anglia.

4　The Beveridge Report (commissioned in 1941 and published in 1942) was only the most evident example of planning for the rebuilding of post-war Britain.

5　*Placing and Management of Building Contracts: The Simon Committee Report*, 1944. Tom Every served on the Simon Committee.

6　Selective tendering was not introduced generally until the 1960s.

7　Langdon died in 1954 and the offices all changed their titles to Langdon & Every in or around 1956.

Chapter Six

Developing Internationally

Much like branch offices in the UK, international networks of quantity surveying firms only emerged after the Second World War. There were, however, pioneering individuals who established firms in territories of the British Empire in the 1920s and 1930s. Quantity surveying is essentially a British invention and its international expansion has tended to be in areas which have strong UK connections or are English speaking or both.

The Irish part of the firm is the oldest part of what is now Davis Langdon & Seah International (DLSI), started by Benjamin Patterson in Dublin in 1860. Two other parts of the firm predate the Second World War: in South Africa, started by Bertram Farrow in Johannesburg in 1922, only three years after Horace Langdon established his practice in London; and in Singapore, started by David Waters and Eric Watson in 1934. The offices that emerged after the War fall into two main groups: those started by Horace W Langdon & Every in the 1940s and those started in the 1950s or later, mostly by British expatriates.

Origins and Early Years

Ireland

On 1 January 1860 Benjamin Patterson, aged 23, set up in practice as an architect, civil engineer and quantity surveyor in a room in his mother's house in Dublin. He had just completed an architectural apprenticeship and, in parallel, had undertaken a Diploma in Civil Engineering at Trinity College Dublin though for the rest of his career he would concentrate on quantity

Portumna Castle, TN Deane.
Courtesy Gillman Collection, Irish
Architectural Archive.

surveying. This one man business was the start of what was to become Patterson Kempster and Shortall (PKS) and, more recently, Davis Langdon PKS.[1] The photograph opposite is of Portumna Castle, designed by TN Deane, for which Patterson measured quantities in 1861.

Patterson was joined by John Kempster in 1872 and the firm became Patterson & Kempster. From the mid-1870s it was one of the pre-eminent firms in Dublin. In 1890, a question was posed in the House of Commons to the Secretary of the Treasury suggesting, in essence, that Patterson & Kempster had a disproportionate share of surveying services on public works in Ireland. The answer, tellingly, was that, over the previous five years, it had received the same amount in fees (£1,600) as the other seven firms employed by the Board of Works together; it concluded with a comment "that the Board employ this firm because they have confidence in them."

In the early 1920s, Patterson & Kempster prepared claims for damage to a number of public buildings and private houses as a result of civil unrest. The British government had undertaken to compensate owners for damage to property during the Sinn Fein revolt and quantity surveyors were employed to assess claims. Interestingly, Horace Langdon undertook similar work in Ireland at the time but, so far as we know, there was no connection between the firms.

In 1970, Patterson & Kempster merged with FD Shortall & Partners and Patterson Kempster & Shortall was formed.

South Africa

The origins of the firm in South Africa came soon after the foundation of the South African Institute of Quantity Surveyors in 1908 and the formal establishment of the Union of South Africa in 1910, as a British colony. Bertram Farrow started his articles as a quantity surveyor in the UK in 1914 but these were interrupted by the First World War. He subsequently qualified as a member of the Institution of Surveyors, forerunner of the Royal Institution of Chartered Surveyors, in 1922 and set up in practice in Johannesburg. At that time there were 26 members of the UK Institution (not just quantity surveyors) in the whole of South Africa and only five in Johannesburg; there were less than 50 members of the South African Institute; and there may, of course, have been dual membership.[2]

In 1933, Farrow was joined by Donald Laing and the firm was renamed Farrow & Laing. They were joined by William Alexander McKechnie some time after and the firm changed its name to Farrow Laing & McKechnie in the late 1930s.[3]

Top: All Saints Church, Raheny, Dublin.
Courtesy the Irish Architectural Archive.
Bottom: Standard Bank, Pretoria,
Stuck & Harrison.

Singapore

The Singapore office has two dates of origin, one as Waters & Watson in
1934 and the other as Horace W Langdon & Every (Far East) after the
Second World War, but they are connected. Among the staff in London
in the early 1930s were Frank Angell, who had been articled to Langdon
in 1922, and Eric Watson who had joined the firm prior to that. In 1932,
Watson resigned to take up a post with a building contractor in Singapore.
After Watson had been in Singapore for some time he met David Waters,
another quantity surveyor in government service, and the two set up in
practice as Waters & Watson. In 1936 Frank Angell went out to Singapore
with the Air Ministry. He met up again with Watson who introduced him
to Waters and, shortly after his contract with the Ministry was complete, he
joined them in practice. For a brief time the firm was called Waters Watson
& Angell.

Seah Mong Hee was born in 1918 in Hainan, an island belonging to China
in the Gulf of Tongking. In 1930, he left with his father for Johore Bahru
in the British colony of Malaya and, when they were established, the rest of
the family joined them. His father worked for a colonial administrator who
took an interest in, and encouraged, young Seah's education. In 1935, having
passed his Cambridge school certificate, he joined Waters & Watson and
started studying for the external examinations of the Surveyors' Institution.
He passed his final examination in 1940 and became the first Chinese
qualified member of the Institution.[4] Seah spent the Japanese occupation
in Singapore.

The partners and staff of Farrow & Laing in 1937
(McKechnie, Farrow and Laing are third, fourth
and fifth from the left in the front row).

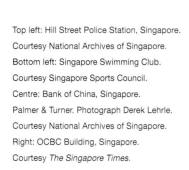

Top left: Hill Street Police Station, Singapore.
Courtesy National Archives of Singapore.
Bottom left: Singapore Swimming Club.
Courtesy Singapore Sports Council.
Centre: Bank of China, Singapore.
Palmer & Turner. Photograph Derek Lehrle.
Courtesy National Archives of Singapore.
Right: OCBC Building, Singapore.
Courtesy *The Singapore Times*.

In 1939 Angell was called up into the Royal Engineers and, at about the same time, Waters & Watson joined the newly-formed Singapore Defence Force. The practice continued but, when the Japanese invaded Singapore in 1942, the office was closed, Waters & Watson were taken prisoner and the local staff dispersed. Angell, however, was evacuated from Singapore and saw war service in a number of theatres in Asia.[5]

After their capture, Waters was taken to Japan and died there; Watson was sent to work on the notorious Burma Railway, survived and was repatriated to the UK shortly after the war ended. He and Angell, separately, both rejoined HWL&E in 1945. After a few months, they talked to Tom Every about returning to Singapore and he suggested that they open up an office as Horace W Langdon & Every. They jumped at the chance and were back in Singapore in 1946, contacting former staff, including their senior and recently qualified assistant, Seah Mong Hee, and establishing the new office.

Horace Langdon was the first London partner to visit the office in Singapore, in 1947 and Tom Every in the following year and that set a pattern for regular visits by the senior partners.

The photograph (overleaf) was probably taken in 1951 or 1952 and it may well have been an office event including spouses and non-members of the firm, possibly clients or colleagues. Sitting in the front row, from the right, there are Seah Mong Hee, Eric Watson and Frank Angell (the local partners),

and Horace Langdon and Giles Every, Tom Every's son. The two gentlemen on the left are unidentified.

Seah Mong Hee became a partner in 1949. Frank Angell returned to the UK to become a partner in the Southampton office in 1956, and finally retired in 1970. Eric Watson died while visiting the Cameron Highlands in 1956; he did not have good health after his experiences under the Japanese. With Angell's and Watson's departures, Seah Mong Hee became senior partner in the Far East. A few years after Langdon's death, the "Horace W" was dropped from the firm's name and in the 1960s it became Langdon Every & Seah, partly to lose the specifically geographic, and slightly dated, "Far East" suffix and partly to recognise local participation in the business.

Kuala Lumpur
An office in Kuala Lumpur was opened in 1947 to handle work for the Royal Air Force but its early years were relatively quiet. In 1958, Mike McLeod, a recent recruit from England was sent to revive the firm's activities. The office was reopened to handle the new University of Malaya; the architects for the first stages were Palmer & Turner. For a few years, Palmer & Turner and the Public Works Department (PWD) were the firm's main sources of work.

In 1968 Nicholas Chong, then the second most senior QS in the PWD and the fourth RICS qualified Chinese quantity surveyor, was invited to join the partnership, effectively to replace McLeod, who returned to the UK.[6] Chong

Group photograph of the Singapore office in the early 1950s.

98   **Thinking Big** A History of Davis Langdon

subsequently invited Baharrudin (Din) Zainal to join in 1974 and from then
on leadership in Malaysia was with Malaysian partners.

Hong Kong

Today, Hong Kong is the longest established office in China although,
when opened and for its first 49 years, it was part of the British Empire,
relinquishing its colonial status only in 1997. In 1948, the local partners
in Singapore, Angell and Watson, persuaded Tom Every that they should
open an office in Hong Kong. Dick Holmes was sent with the promise
of War Department and PWD work which, in the event did not transpire.

The office struggled in its early days until Holmes acquired as clients the
Hong Kong Housing Authority and Hong Kong Land, the largest private
development company. The office took off and by the 1950s was earning
more than Singapore. It went from strength to strength through the next
three decades, under British leadership and with a significant British staff
complement. In 1980, ML Ku became the first Chinese partner and the change
to Chinese leadership and staffing accelerated the growth of the offices.

The Middle East

In 1946, at around the same time as Frank Angell and Eric Watson were
returning to Singapore, Tom Every, himself, travelled to Persia to prepare
a report for the Anglo-Iranian Oil Company and started the firm's presence in
the Middle East. HWL&E seconded staff to Anglo Iranian for a number of
years, interrupted by their emergency evacuation in 1951, during the Abadan
Oil Crisis.[7]

The first Horace W Langdon & Every (Arabian Gulf) office was opened in Kuwait in 1948 to undertake work for the ruling family. The country was relatively wealthy as a trading port and the first shipment of oil had been exported in 1946, it was under British protection and the ruler was keen that it should be developed and modernised. Initial work comprised residential and educational projects and major infrastructure, including a desalination plant. In the 1950s, the firm moved to Aden and took over a small local practice and in the 1960s the headquarters moved to Bahrain, where there has been a presence ever since. At the end of the 1960s, the professional staff was around a dozen strong, all expatriates.

New Zealand

After service in the Royal Air Force in the Second World War, George Knapman set up as a quantity surveyor in Fiji, then part of the British

Top left: Bank in Doha.

Bottom left: Salmaniya Medical Centre, Bahrein.

Right: Copy of Alan Berryman's expulsion letter from the nationalised National Iranian Oil Company, 1951.

Empire. He was a frequent visitor to Auckland in New Zealand and, in 1953, won a major commission for quantity surveying services on a new factory for Alcan (the Aluminium Company of Canada). On the project he met Barry Clark, a quantity surveyor working for Fletchers, the contractors, and in 1954 the firm of Knapman Clark was formed. Knapman did not give up his practice in Fiji immediately but his attention was on developing the business in New Zealand and it was eventually taken over by the managers there.

Knapman Clark prospered and by the late 1950s had offices in Auckland and Wellington. Wellington, then as now, was important for government work and it was increasingly desirable that the firm had a resident partner. The partners eventually appointed Alan Pankhurst, a relative of the suffragette, in 1960.

Australia

Steve Beattie, a British quantity surveyor, sailed with his family to Australia as an assisted immigrant in 1955. He was sponsored by Wakeman Trower & Partners (now the WT Partnership) and worked for them for a few years in Melbourne. It was a busy time for the construction industry and quantity surveyors and Beattie and a WT colleague, Ron Prowse, an Australian, decided to set up on their own as Beattie Prowse. The practice expanded into Tasmania but otherwise remained relatively small and local with a speciality in healthcare buildings.

Also in the 1950s, L&E in London were appointed to act as quantity surveyors for the new BP headquarters building on St Kilda Road in Melbourne, designed by Demaine Russell Armstrong Orton and Trundle, and now an apartment building. Tom Every was keen to establish an Australian practice but the traditional UK service and fee levels offered by HWL&E were seriously out of line with Australian practice and the venture was not pursued. Some time later, Mike McLeod visited Australia from Kuala Lumpur with the intention of establishing links with Langdon Every & Seah (LES) in South-East Asia. An informal link with Beattie Prowse was formed but no work followed; the Australian partners were content to maintain a purely Australian practice.

In the 1970s, Beattie Prowse was appointed as quantity surveyor on an Australian Chancery building in Kuala Lumpur and made contact again with LES in Kuala Lumpur. A few years later, Mark Beattie, son of Steve, and Bob Hunt, another young partner in Beattie Prowse, decided that an international link was necessary, not least because the market was difficult in Australia at that time, and reopened discussions with LES. The outcome was a joint venture called Langdon Every Hunt & Beattie, which opened in Sydney in 1983.

USA

Peter Adamson, a UK born quantity surveyor who had done his articles with Franklin & Andrews in the late 1940s, arrived in California via Canada 20 years later and, initially, worked as an estimator for a local contractor. In the early 1970s, he was asked by MDA (Monk Dunstone Associates) to open an office for them in San Francisco and was joined shortly afterwards by Martin Gordon, another young British quantity surveyor who had fallen for San Francisco. In 1974, however, MDA decided to close their San Francisco office and concentrate on the East Coast but both Adamson and Gordon decided to stay in California and, later that year, Adamson got work with architects on an airport project south of San Francisco, checking contractors' estimates. He asked Gordon to join him and Adamson Associates was born.

An office was established in Palo Alto, 45 minutes south of San Francisco because that was where the original work was but, four years later, Gordon opened an office in San Francisco and the firm grew from there. By 1985, the San Francisco office was three times the size of Palo Alto and the firm consolidated in the former location.

The International Firm Today

In 2008, Davis Langdon & Seah International (DLSI), the international firm has over 5,000 staff in 100 offices in 25 countries worldwide. The map overleaf indicates the locations of the offices.

The various member firms of DLSI have a number of corporate structures. The UK was a traditional unlimited partnership until 2004 and is now a Limited Liability Partnership (LLP); most other firms have private company structures although, like the UK, most will have started as traditional partnerships. The Asian firm, for example, is a now a group of companies, each established in accordance with local requirements and circumstances. The rationales for the move from partnership to company are usually some combination of tax advantage and reduced individual liability.

When the UK and Asian firms (DLE and LES) joined together in 1990, the former had a relatively small (around four per cent) share in the latter. It was decided later in the decade that this shareholding should be abandoned and that there should be cross-shareholdings designed to ensure a neutral allocation of profits between the two groups over the medium term (three years). In the event, this took endless amounts of discussion and calculation, of the definition of profits, exchange rates, tax regimes, etc., to agree allocations, all

Top: Steve Beattie

Bottom: The Australian Chancery Building, Kuala Lumpur, Leong Thian & Rakan Rakan in association with Joyce Nankivell Associates Pty Ltd. Copyright Pertubuhan Akitek Malaysia, 1987, reproduced from *Post-Merdeka Architecture*.

of which was eventually decided to be ultimately pointless since the intent was that neither party should benefit or lose by the arrangement.

The structure that was selected to address the problem was a Swiss *verein*, a form of business organisation comprising a number of independent jurisdictions each of which has limited liability *vis a vis* the others.[8] The *verein* was also the structure that accommodated the Australian firm that had been in joint venture with LES and it would take in other firms in other regions. It was the basis for the international firm, DLSI; individual national firms maintained their own form and structure and separately joined the *verein*.

The main purpose of the *verein* was to establish common standards (for example, IT, professional procedures, etc.) across the international practice without the complications of shared management, ownership and finances. Its main disadvantage, particularly in the longer term, is its lack of corporate 'glue' but it has the advantages of simplicity of establishment and operation and non-controversial business relationships. It was probably the right model at the time.

Asia

When L&E and DLE merged in 1988, the associated firm of L&E in Asia, Langdon Every & Seah (LES) was the 'jewel in the crown' as far as DB&E was concerned. LES had offices in Singapore, Hong Kong, Indonesia, Malaysia, Brunei, the Philippines and a total staff of 657, almost half of them in Hong Kong. There was also the joint venture company in Australia. And it worked extensively, although it had no permanent offices, in mainland China.

The merger enabled DB&E to make a leap from a large UK national practice to a major international force in quantity surveying, at least nominally (LES was, in fact substantially owned by the partners based in Asia and the links with the L&E in the UK were neither as close nor as active as they could have been). For good practical reasons, the alliance of DLE and LES was not finalised until 1990; when it was, the international organisation created, was unquestionably the largest group of quantity surveyors in the world.

The Asian partners knew about the proposed UK merger in 1987; they were informed, rather than consulted but, in any case, they were broadly supportive. It had no immediate management or financial implications for them; they had been self-managing for many years and L&E's equity and profit share in LES was small. An interesting side-attraction of the merger to the Asian partners and its presentation was that they could now be perceived as part of an international group, not as a branch of a British firm, an important distinction for at least some partners.

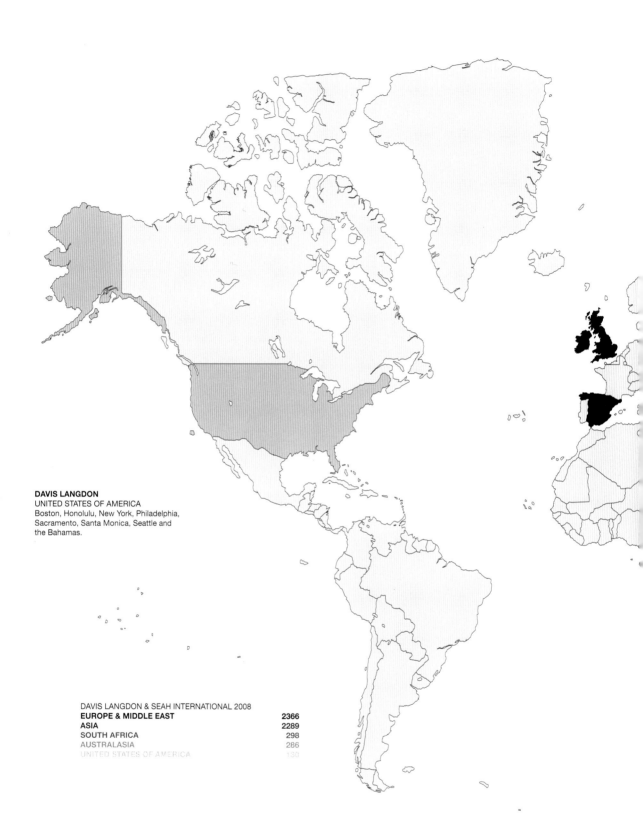

DAVIS LANGDON
UNITED STATES OF AMERICA
Boston, Honolulu, New York, Philadelphia,
Sacramento, Santa Monica, Seattle and
the Bahamas.

DAVIS LANGDON & SEAH INTERNATIONAL 2008
EUROPE & MIDDLE EAST   **2366**
ASIA   **2289**
SOUTH AFRICA   298
AUSTRALASIA   286
UNITED STATES OF AMERICA   130

DAVIS LANGDON
EUROPE AND THE MIDDLE EAST
England: London, Birmingham, Bristol, Cambridge, Leeds, Liverpool, Maidstone, Manchester, Milton Keynes, Norwich, Oxford, Peterborough, Plymouth, Southampton, Stevenage **Wales:** Cardiff **Scotland:** Aberdeen, Edinburgh, Glasgow **Ireland:** Belfast, Cork, Dublin, Galway, Limerick **Russia:** Moscow **Spain:** Barcelona **Lebanon:** Beirut **Bahrain:** Manama **UAE:** Dubai, Abu Dhabi **Qatar:** Doha **Croatia:** Zagreb

DAVIS LANGDON & SEAH
ASIA
Brunei: Bandar Seri Begawan **China:** Beijing, Chongqing, Guangzhou, Hong Kong, Macau, Shanghai, Shenzhen, Tianjin, Wuhan **India:** Bangalore, Chennai, Delhi, Hyderabad, Mumbai **Indonesia:** Bali, Jakarta, Surabaya **Japan:** Tokyo, Nagoya **Kazakhstan:** Almaty **South Korea:** Seoul **Pakistan:** Karachi **Malaysia:** Johor Bahru, Kota Kinabalu, Kuala Lumpur, Kuching, Penang **Philippines:** Manila **Singapore:** Singapore **Thailand:** Bangkok **Vietnam:** Hanoi, Ho Chi Minh City

DAVIS LANGDON
SOUTH AFRICA
South Africa: Bloemfontein, Cape Town, Durban, George, Johannesburg, Klerksdorp, Pietermaritzburg, Port Shepstone, Pretoria, Richards Bay, Somerset West, Stellenbosch, Tygerberg, Vanderbijlpark **Botswana:** Gaborone

DAVIS LANGDON
AUSTRALASIA
Australia: Adelaide, Brisbane, Cairns, Canberra, Darwin, Hobart, Melbourne, Perth, Sydney, Townsville
New Zealand: Auckland, Wellington

LES was essentially a single partnership across seven territories and 12 offices, although each territory had its own local structures. LES had, and DLS has, no head office; the senior partner in 1988 was Nicholas Chong, based in Kuala Lumpur in Malaysia. His successor, Seah Choo Meng, son of Seah Mong Hee, retired and Joseph Lee, senior partner in Hong Kong, took over the role in 2009. Since 1946, therefore, the senior partners have been based in Singapore, Kuala Lumpur, Singapore, again, and now Hong Kong. DLS in 2009 has around 2,300 people in 30 offices in 12 countries.

In detail, the DLS structure in 2008 is complicated but holding to the overarching idea of a single partnership is helpful. There are 16 international directors in DLS who all have an interest in all offices; there are also local directors who only have an interest in a single office or territory.

Singapore

The office in Singapore is the longest established office in Asia. It has 300 staff and four international partners. It also controls operations in Indonesia, Vietnam, India, Korea and Kazakhstan.

For more than 70 years there has always been at least one member of the Seah family in the firm. The first, Seah Mong Hee, joined Waters & Watson in the 1930s, was a partner in Horace W Langdon & Every from 1949 and became senior partner of Langdon Every & Seah in 1956; he retired in 1975 and died in 2009. Seah Choo Meng joined the firm in 1968, became a partner in 1976, senior partner in South-East Asia in 1998 and retired in 2008. The Seah family connection continues with Seah Hsiu Min, Choo Meng's son.

Malaysia

There were five main offices of the firm in Malaysia in 2008, Kuala Lumpur, Penang, Johor Bahru, Kota Kinabalu and Kuching, with four international partners and around 200 staff. The firm practices as DLS and JUBM (Juru Ukur Bahan Malaysia). JUBM is an entirely Malaysian entity undertaking work for the Malaysian government and some private clients; DLS tends to work for foreign clients, for example, investors from Hong Kong or Singapore or, increasingly, further afield. The government of Malaysia has actually promoted Malaysian firms and, specifically, ethnic Malay owned firms since the 1970s.

Brunei

The State of Brunei is now an independent country but prior to 1984, it was a British Protectorate and DLS has had an office there since 1965. There are now 120 people in Brunei and 16 people in Sarawak. Most of the work is related to the petrochemical industry and largely for Shell Petroleum or the

government. There was a number of reasons for the move into Brunei but, as usual, the firm was pursuing work with clients and designers it knew.

Malcolm Smithson was the first resident member of staff in Bandar Seri Begawan, the capital, initially mainly doing building work; he was joined by Tony Teoh who subsequently spent most of his career with DLS in Brunei: he was an assistant QS in the 1960s, a senior surveyor in the 1970s, a manager in 1980 and a partner in 1983; he retired in 2002. His son, Justin, is now resident partner in Brunei and an international partner of DLS.

China and Hong Kong SAR

China, with nine offices throughout the mainland and in Hong Kong and Macao, is by far the largest territory in DLS. There are five international partners and a total of some 850 staff, 350 in Hong Kong. DLS's first project in mainland China was the Silver Bay Harbour and Port Facilities at Zhuhai, Guangdong Province, in 1983, just across the then border with Hong Kong. Their first office in China was in Beijing in 1985 to work on the China World Trade Center project. The Shanghai office was opened a year later. An office was opened in Guangzhou City in 1992. Offices were opened in Shenzhen in 2001, although they had been working in and around the city since 1992; in Chongqing and Wuhan in 2005; and in Tianjin and Shenyang in 2007. The Macao office opened in 2008.

Other Asian offices

An office was opened in Jakarta, in Indonesia, in 1972, in Bangkok, in Thailand, in 1987 and in Manila, in the Philippines, in 1990. The office in

Left: Ceremonial Royal Barge for
the Sultan of Brunei, Ho Kwong Yew.
Right: Refurbishment of Raffles Hotel, Singapore
Architect 61 Pte Ltd.

CCTV Headquarters, Beijing,
Rem Koolhaas, OMA.

Manila was opened to handle the firm's work on the Asian Development Bank (ADB) headquarters building, designed by Skidmore Owings & Merrill.

While working on the ADB project, it became evident that a cadre of well educated, English speaking engineers was available that could be trained to become quantity surveyors and that a low cost base could be established for outsourcing the preparation of bills of quantities from around the region but particularly from higher cost locations. The operation was taken very seriously and a structured training course was delivered by DLS personnel. Manila still acts as a bill of quantities and documentation 'factory' and now includes some UK offices in its customers.

Some ten years after the North Vietnamese army had defeated South Vietnam and the Americans had left Saigon in disarray, the Vietnamese government decided to rethink their national development policy and introduce an 'open door' strategy called "*Doi Moi*". This was intended to encourage foreign investment and to move, albeit hesitantly, towards a market economy. DLS were asked to go to Vietnam by existing clients from around the region who wished to build offices, factories, hotels and residential developments. These were all joint venture projects with, essentially, the local partner (usually public sector) providing the land and the foreign partner providing the capital. The foreign partner usually preferred to bring their construction team with them and that often included LES.

Country	Year of Establishment	Offices
Singapore	1934	Singapore
Malaysia	1947	Kuala Lumpur (1947), Penang (1989), Johor Bahru (1991), Kuching (1981), Kota Kinabalu (1969)
Hong Kong/China	1949	Shanghai (1986), Beijing (1985), Guanzhou (1992), Shenzen (2001), Chongquing (2002), Wuhan (2002), Macau (2005), Tianjin (2007), Shenyang (2007), Chengdu (2007), Foshan (2007)
Brunei	1965	Bandar Seri Begawan, Kuala Belait
Indonesia	1972	Jakarta, Bali, Surabya
Thailand	1984	Bangkok
Vietnam	1995	Hanoi, Ho Chin Minh City
Philippines	1990	Manila
South Korea	2000	Seoul
India	2004	Bangalore, Mumbai, Hyderabad Delhi, Chennai
Pakistan	2007	Karachi
Kazakhstan	2008	Almaty
Japan	2008	Tokyo

Summary

Asia

It is interesting to consider the mix of, and reasons for, expatriate and local staff and partners in the Asian offices. Local QS courses were not introduced until the 1960s and, prior to that, the only routes to qualification were correspondence courses or going to the UK and studying and, possibly, working there. For the first you needed encouragement and application; for the second, these and financial resources. Seah Mong Hee was an outstanding early example of the first, qualifying in 1940. Nicholas Chong exemplifies the second; he won a Malayan government scholarship to study in London in 1956 and did articles with John Leaning & Sons and, in 1961, was to become only the second local partner in the firm.

In 1963, Singapore Polytechnic introduced a five year quantity surveying course so the first graduates did not emerge until the late 1960s. It is also the case that, until the 1970s, many of the firm's clients were represented

Table showing DLS offices in 2008.

by expatriates, government, foreign banks and trading houses. For all these reasons, until the 1960s, there was a need for expatriate staff. It took a little longer for local surveyors with partnership qualities to come through. Nowadays there is only a nominal number of expatriate partners. Interestingly, however, in new territories for the firm, offices are often headed by expatriates.

Tom Every very much controlled the development of Langdon & Every Far East in the early days after the Second World War and, after Horace Langdon's death in 1954 was the sole UK shareholder until his son Giles joined the UK practice in 1963. Since then ownership of the Far East practice has moved progressively towards the local partners.

Seah Mong Hee was succeeded by Peter Sanderson. Seah had been a partner from 1949 and senior partner since 1956. He was in Nicholas Chong's words "The patriarch of quantity surveying in Asia and the *pater familias* of the firm." Under Seah's leadership, the offices in the Far East were very much a single firm. Under Peter Sanderson and then Nicholas Chong, who took over as senior partner in 1979, the different offices began to project themselves as autonomous in their own areas of operation.

Although different territories had their good years and bad years, LES saw more or less steady growth in revenues and profits from the 1960s overall until the East Asian crisis in 1997 when investment generally slowed to a standstill. The firm withdrew from Indonesia and Vietnam and retrenched in other territories but has since returned to both countries.

The central area of Beirut, for Solidere, the public/private organisation responsible for the post-war rebuilding of the city.

The Middle East

The Langdon & Every (Arabian Gulf) office moved from Aden to Bahrain in 1965, Doha in Qatar was opened in 1974, and Dubai in the United Arab Emirates in 1979. Between the 1960s and the 1980s a range of projects were undertaken in the Gulf and in Iraq.

A Davis Belfield & Everest office was opened in Kuwait in the early 1980s to undertake mainly petrochemical related quantity surveying work for a number of oil companies, including the Kuwait National Petroleum Company and by the late 1980s, there were almost 30 people based in Kuwait. Staff numbers had reduced to six by August 1990 when the Iraqi army invaded Kuwait. Two people were on leave and out of the country and three others managed to leave the country by road into Saudi Arabia but the manager, John Gowland, and his wife remained. Gowland was 'rounded up' by the Iraqis, his wife was deported to the UK and he was then taken to northern Iraq as part of Saddam Hussein's 'human shield'. After Edward Heath's intervention, he was released and returned to the UK five months later.

In 1990, an old friend of Derek Johnson, (a London-based project management partner who went on to become the managing partner in the Middle East), Muhyiddin Itani, a Lebanese quantity surveyor who had spent many years working in Saudi Arabia, decided to return home to Beirut. The two discussed prospects in Lebanon, prepared a business plan and, with the approval of the management board, agreed to set up a joint venture company in Lebanon. The firm already had experience on the reconstruction of central Beirut and saw Lebanon as not only a good market but also as a source of good qualified local staff.

In the late 1990s, an office was established in Cairo to manage a series of projects for Middle East clients in Egypt. The projects went well and some other work for international clients was secured but it was difficult to sustain an expatriate based office in Egypt and it was eventually closed in 2004.

The Middle East offices now operate as part of a combined UK, Europe and Middle East region.

Australia and New Zealand

The creation of DLSI in 1990 brought Australia into the new international practice through the Sydney joint venture, Langdon Every Hunt & Beattie

and Beattie Prowse was replaced by Davis Langdon & Beattie, with offices in Melbourne, Sydney and Tasmania; in 1992 it became Davis Langdon Australia. Linkages were made with Eric Ash in Brisbane and Ian Silver & Associates in Perth; initially these were renamed Davis Langdon & Ash and Davis Langdon & Silver but shortly after they became Davis Langdon Australia.

Australia has a federal structure and some decisions are made by public and private clients at national level but most are made locally, at State level. This means that a national practice needs to have at least one office in each State capital. The firm has ten offices and over 200 staff in Australia. Not only does Davis Langdon Australasia have offices nationwide, it also has a national structure, and all equity directors are directors of Davis Langdon Australia.

Davis Langdon New Zealand is currently around 60 strong, with offices in Auckland, Wellington and Christchurch and operates as a single partnership across all offices. Approximately 50 per cent of the staff in Auckland is expatriate, mainly British.

The relationship between Knapman Clark in New Zealand and Davis Langdon Australia dates back to 1998. Davis Langdon New Zealand (DLNZ) joined DLSI in their own right and simultaneously entered into an equity swap relationship with DLA (currently DLA owns 15 per cent of DLNZ and DLNZ owns five per cent of DLA). The partners/directors of both firms believe that the cross-shareholding increases mutual interest, although, in practice, very little money changes hands. Australia and New Zealand combined have a turnover of $US 56 million.

Above: The Australian board. From left to right: Gary Boyd, Mark Beattie, Bob Hunt, David Abraham (non-executive), Brett Clabburn, Ian Jackson.

Opposite top: Green Point Stadium, Cape Town, South Africa. Courtesy of design by gmp international architects and engineers.

Opposite centre left: Tunnel towards Sandton, Gautrain Rapid Rail Link, Gauteng Province, South Africa, Gautrain Architects Joint Venture.

Opposite bottom left: State Hockey Centre, Sydney Olympic Site, Australia, HOK Sport.

Opposite bottom right: Eureka Tower, Melbourne, Fender Katsalidis Architects.

Africa

The South African practice joined the DLSI *verein* in 1999 as Davis Langdon Farrow Laing; it changed its name to Davis Langdon Africa in 2004 and finally, in 2006, to plain Davis Langdon. There were long standing links with the UK. Nick Davis, UK senior partner, 1993–1998, worked there in the 1960s and Chris du Toit and Alastair Collins worked and were partners in both practices. The background to the links were individual connections, a common heritage and similar professional practices but, for many years, relations were necessarily distant, largely as a result of international opposition to the apartheid regime in South Africa. Obstacles to closer links were removed with the end of apartheid between 1990 and 1993 and the election of Nelson Mandela as President of a new South Africa in 1994.

In 2008 Davis Langdon Africa had 20 offices, just over 300 people and a turnover of $US 30 million.

L&E worked in West Africa in the 1970s, in Nigeria, where they established an informal relationship with a local firm of quantity surveyors, QuEss Partnership, but this was not an area of expansion for the firm, unlike a number of their competitors. Although there was a major British presence in Africa, even after independence in the 1950s and 1960s, economic activity and progress did not compare with, say, Singapore, Hong Kong and Malaysia and, from the 1970s, exchange control issues and political uncertainties made work in most sub-Saharan African states difficult. The principal exception was, of course, South Africa but that was itself problematic, particularly in the apartheid years.

America

Both DB&E and L&E had experience of working in the USA before they merged, including L&E's advisory services on the British Airways terminal at New York (Kennedy) airport, designed by Gollins Melvin Ward. The work tended to be with long standing international clients or design practices with which the firm had close links. Prior to the 1980s there were never any serious efforts to establish a presence in North America. In the 1980s and 1990s there were conversations with a number of US practices, usually with UK origins, but nothing came of these.

In the mid-1990s, Davis Langdon was asked to work with Foster & Partners on a new medical research centre at Stanford University in Palo Alto,

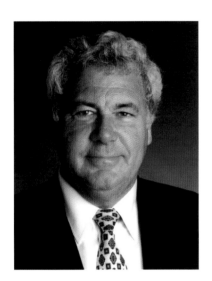

California. Unfamiliar with the role of the UK quantity surveyor, Adamson Associates, a local firm of cost consultants was appointed by the University to work with DLE. The two firms had met before. Paul Morrell, looking for local knowledge in the USA had tracked down Martin Gordon at Adamson Associates in San Francisco. When Gordon was asked if he could help, his response was "Sure", not "How do we share the fee?" or "Whose Professional Indemnity Insurance is at risk?" Both men decided the two firms' 'cultures' were compatible. The Stanford job went well and Morrell suggested a closer tie up. The response was positive and Adamsons joined the DLSI *verein* in 1999 as Davis Langdon Adamson.

From their origins in and around San Francisco, Adamson Associates expanded into Santa Monica, Los Angeles, in 1987, to take on board another British expatriate quantity surveyor, Nick Butcher, and opened offices in Sacramento, 1994, and Seattle, 1995. Peter Adamson died in 1992 and the firm carried on headed by Gordon, and, more recently, by Butcher. In 2002, then part of DLSI, an office was opened in New York City, followed by offices in Boston and Philadelphia and, most recently, Honolulu. The firm currently has staff of 120 and turnover of over $20 million. In 2005 Davis Langdon Adamson dropped the Adamson to become Davis Langdon.

Europe

The Irish practice of Patterson Kempster & Shortall (PKS) formally joined Davis Langdon in 2002 after many years of informal links and joint projects. It is now part of the UK, Europe and the Middle East region. It has four offices, Cork, Dublin, Galway and Limerick.

In the 1990s, efforts were made to establish a network of offices in mainland Europe. Enthusiasm following the merger, recession in the UK and the hoped-for benefits of the Single European Market all encouraged these efforts. Links with Edetco, based in Catalonia, had been established in the 1980s when the firm had worked with James Stirling and Michael Wilford, on the redevelopment of the Abando railway station in Bilbao. Links with project manager Walter Weiss were long-standing and included collaboration on the Staatsgalerie in Stuttgart, also with Stirling & Wilford. And contact was made with Keith Copper, a sole practioner British expatriate QS in Rome. In all three cases, joint venture companies were established but only Davis Langdon Edetco survives.

A French practice was established in Paris as Davis Langdon Economistes, the majority of which is owned by the UK practice. This operated for a number of

Top: Martin Gordon.
Bottom: Nick Butcher.

years and undertook a range of work but was never a commercial success. It was eventually closed in 2006. The message from these ventures into mainland Western Europe was that it is difficult to establish a specialist cost consultancy in these markets. Cost consultancy is often provided by design consultancies and is in any case not a premium service; it is difficult to break into the local market with a largely unknown service; and there is probably insufficient international business to justify a permanent presence.

The continuing link with Edetco in Catalonia suggests another approach. Edetco is a technical architect *(aparajador)* and a project and construction manager as well as a cost consultant. Its cost consultancy services, while sophisticated, are an added feature of its mainly management services. Davis Langdon Edetco can present itself as "more than just a quantity surveyor" in the Spanish market.

Later in the decade and early in the 2000s, a number of projects were undertaken in Central and Eastern Europe. Recently a joint venture was established in Moscow and an office opened in Zagreb, Croatia.

Commentary

The twentieth century saw quantity surveying become an established part of the construction industry in Britain and develop progressively internationally, particularly but not exclusively in the English speaking world. The Empire was still an important element of British political and economic life in the first half of the century. British presence in the Far East, the Middle East, Africa and elsewhere provided opportunities for British firms and individuals to widen their activities and areas of operation. Most, although not all, of the origins of Davis Langdon's present day offices lie in the years before and just after the Second World War.

More than half of Davis Langdon & Seah International is based outside the UK and, broadly, this has been the case since the merger between L&E and DB&E in 1988. The table opposite indicates the distribution, by staff numbers and revenues, of the firm's principal operations between 2003 and 2008.

Top: The Davis Langdon PKS Board of Directors, from left to right: Paul Mitchell, Norman Craig, Donn O'Shaughnessy, Martin Andrews, John O'Regan, Peter Flint.
Bottom: Offaly County Council Offices, Tullamore, ABK Architects.

The *verein* was a key enabler in creating the DLSI that existed in 2008. It helped resolve the relationship between the UK and Asian firms; it allowed the Australasian, American and African firms to join the group without complicated legal and financial negotiations; and it provided a framework for the European and Middle East practice. It did, however, tend to create geographical and practice silos and did not encourage development of

Region	2003		2008	
	Staff	Revenues	Staff	Revenues
Europe and the Middle East	1,210	145.0	2,408	408.8
Asia	1,045	37.0	2,332	99.2
Australia and New Zealand	175	16.4	283	56.3
Africa	215	10.7	305	29.5
USA	56	9.0	120	22.0
Global Total	2,701	218.1	5,448	616.8

a genuinely global, rather than merely an international practice. There is currently an initiative to link the various parts of groups more closely.

1   A full account of the origins of PKS is in *One Hundred Years of Quantity Surveying, the Annals of Patterson and Kempster* by Gordon Aston, a partner of PKS, published by Hinds Publishing, Dublin, 2007.

2   The South African Institute was affiliated with the Surveyors' Institution, the so-called Home Institute, in 1925, although the South African Institute, of course, was only for quantity surveyors. The South African Institute was replaced by the Chapter of South African Quantity Surveyors in 1927 and the Chapter was replaced by the Association of South African Quantity Surveyors, the current institutional format, in 1970.

3   It reverted to Farrow Laing & Partners when Farrow Laing & McKechnie merged with Lane Wherry & Hattinghe in 1976. Lane Wherry & Hattinghe was founded in Bloemfontein in 1946.

4   This was a striking achievement. A future senior partner of the firm, Nicholas Chong, was the fourth qualified member of the RICS in Asia. He qualified 25 years after Seah Mong Hee.

5   After the war he wrote a memoire that was published in the *Journal of the Royal Engineers,* "Escape from Singapore" (in four parts), Major Francis L Angell RE.

6   McLeod returned to the UK in 1970 after spending six months in Hong Kong and became a partner in L&E UK. He became senior partner in 1987 and joint senior partner of DLE in 1988. He retired in 1993.

7   In 1951, the Iranian government announced its intention to nationalise Anglo Iranian.

8   *Verein* is a German term for "association" or "union". In application it is similar to the Anglo-American voluntary association. The Swiss *verein* structure has been adopted by a number of major international professional services firms including, for example, Deloitte Touche Tohmatsu and Baker & McKenzie.

Table showing DLSI staff and revenues, 2003 and 2008.

Chapter Seven

From a Traditional to a Modern Firm

Two years after the 1988 merger, Davis Langdon & Everest (DLE), and the rest of the UK construction industry slid into the worst recession since the Second World War. It was to be more than ten years before 1990 levels of construction demand were recovered. The graph below shows the trends in output from 1988 to 2003: collapse, recovery, a slight downturn at the millennium followed by steady growth.[1]

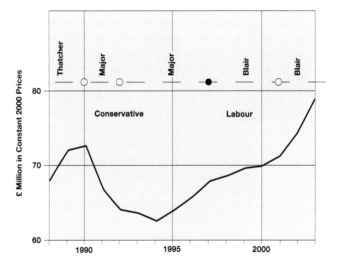

The period started with a Conservative government headed by John Major (he replaced Margaret Thatcher in November 1990) and ended in the second administration of Tony Blair. There were elections in 1992, which Major won, in 1997, Blair's first victory, and in 2001, his second. Although Major ended 13 years of Thatcher's premiership and Blair ended 18 years of Conservative government, key aspects of policy that had been established in the 1980s were left largely unchanged. These included confidence in the market and the private sector; continuation of privatisation and development of the idea of public private partnerships as a way of procuring 'public' facilities; and deregulation: 'rolling back the state'.

Like previous post-war construction 'busts', the chief culprit of the 1990/1991 one was the abrupt halt of excessive private commercial investment. There was a downturn in public spending but not to the extent of the private downturn. The graph opposite is based on new orders for construction rather than output, that is, it records work placed rather than work produced so it is more volatile than output (output is a mixture of new work and work in progress, its trend is, therefore, smoothed). New orders also omit repair and maintenance, which tends to be more stable in volume over time and, again, tends to have a smoothing effect.

Graph showing construction output by all agencies, 1988 to 2003. Source: Office for National Statistics (ONS).

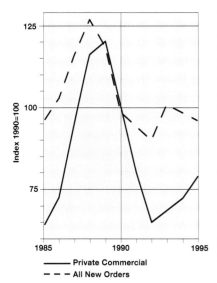

Index 1990=100

125

100

75

1985   1990   1995

——— Private Commercial
— — — All New Orders

The graph shows all new orders and private commercial new orders in constant price terms drawn as an index with 1990 = 100. The peak in all new orders comes earlier than commercial new orders largely because private housing new orders (40 per cent of all new orders) peaked in 1988. The volume of all new orders is similar in 1985 and 1995 with the range over the period being from 90 to 127. The volume of private commercial orders is higher in 1995 than it was in 1985 and the range is much greater, from 66 to 120. Private housing and private commercial new orders represented 64 per cent of all new orders in 1985, 59 per cent in 1990 and 51 per cent in 1995.[2]

The dramatic reduction in new work from the late 1980s led to fierce competition just at the time when fee competition had been generally adopted.[3] Reduced volume of work combined with reduced price levels and competitive fee rates led to dramatic falls in the revenues of professional firms whose income depended largely on *ad valorem* fees.[4] DLE's 1991 fee income of £31 million was not exceeded until 1999, when it was £32.5 million (not adjusted for inflation).

There was a need for firms to simultaneously reduce costs and improve productivity. The results were, initially, early retirements and voluntary redundancies but then compulsory redundancies, a painful process for all concerned. DLE staff numbers dropped by a third between 1990 and 1993. Firms made other cost savings wherever possible: paid overtime was abolished and the allocation of company cars to all qualified staff was progressively phased out. Interestingly, these employment benefits were generally not restored when better times returned. Not surprisingly, a number of old and familiar contracting and consultancy names disappeared in the 1990s.

The new firm of Davis Langdon & Everest was affected by the downturn but to some extent it was better positioned, and perhaps responded better, than many other firms. It still had major long-term contracts running, notably The British Library on Euston Road in London and Sizewell B Power Station on the Suffolk coast, both having started 15 or so years earlier. And there were other prestige projects in hand, including the Queen's Stand at Epsom, designed by Michael Hordern & Partners, the Sackler Gallery at the Royal Academy, designed by Norman Foster, and the Combined Operations Centre at Heathrow and Waterloo International Rail Terminal, both designed by Nicholas Grimshaw & Partners.

Although international work was not traditionally a mainstay of the UK practice, particularly the DB&E part of the firm, many of the architects they worked with were established international names that brought international

Graph showing new orders for construction work, 1985 to 1995. Source: ONS.

projects. The decline in workload in the early 1980s encouraged a number of partners to pursue overseas, particularly European, work to an extent that they had not previously. Projects at this time included the redevelopment of the old Fiat car plant at Lingotto, designed by Renzo Piano, the British Pavilion at the Seville Expo in 1992, designed by Michael Hopkins and the Reichstag in Berlin, designed by Norman Foster.

There were also new projects, large and small, in the UK, notably the Glaxo Research Centre at Stevenage, designed by Sheppard Robson, at one time the largest construction project in Europe; and a project management commission for No 1 Poultry in the City of London, designed by James Stirling & Michael Wilford. And Bupa, the private healthcare provider, carried on developing projects throughout the 1990s.

The industry began to emerge from recession in 1993 and 1994. Changes that had started in the 1980s were now established parts of the landscape including fee competition, simplified pricing documents, management forms of contract, the relative importance of private sector clients and the decline of public building commissions and a continuing reduction of the roles and responsibilities of the architect and the rise of the project manager. The recovery was slow and people, employers and employees, were cautious. The previous three or four years had been traumatic and very few were willing to believe that it was all over.

Mike McLeod and Geoff Trickey, the joint senior partners who had carried through the 1988 merger handed over to a new single senior partner, Nick

Left: Combined Operations Centre, Heathrow, Nicholas Grimshaw & Partners.
Photographer: John Edward Linden/arcaid.co.uk.
Right: Sackler Gallery, Royal Academy, London, Foster & Partners.
Photographer: Roman von Gotz/Bildarchiv Monheim/arcaid.co.uk.

Top left: Lingotto Factory, Turin, Renzo Piano.

Bottom left: Reichstag, Berlin,

Foster & Partners.

Right: No. 1 Poultry, James Stirling

& Michael Wilford.

Davis, in April 1993. To continue a tradition established at the time of the merger, Davis was photographed for the cover of *Building* magazine. McLeod and Trickey had had an eventful five year term, taking in, amongst other things, the end of the 1980s boom, the merger and a major bust. They had also started the business of reorganising the firm. The partners' agreement set the senior partners' tenure at five years, they were both 58, two years younger than the DLE partnership retirement age but both opted to retire immediately.

Davis had been a partner for 27 years and was the son of Owen Davis, the founder of DB&E. He was committed to maintaining the professional standards and traditions of the firm and keen to see it through the tail end of the recession. He was also concerned that the association with the Far East, completed in 1990, was thoroughly bedded in. Davis' style was consensual, an appropriate style for the time.

The environment within which Davis Langdon & Everest operated was changing both externally and internally. External influences came from Europe,

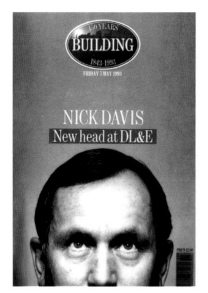

from the British Government and from the private sector. Internal changes partly flowed directly from the merger and partly from these external pressures.

External Changes

To preview the 1990s and beyond, Davis Langdon Consultancy (DLC), the forerunner of Davis Langdon Management Consulting was appointed by the QS Division of the RICS in 1990 to undertake a study of the *Future Role of the Chartered Quantity Surveyor*.[5] The report was published just when the downturn was becoming evident. Its analysis was right about a number of things: that private practice would evolve into large, multiskilled practices and smaller niche practices; that quantity surveyors would move from measurement to management; and that "tomorrow's quantity surveyors would need to be more innovative, more pro-active and more mobile than today's". It also noted that bills of quantities would not disappear but that quantity surveyors would not necessarily be the people who prepared them.

In January 1992, the Single European Market came into existence, following the signature of the Single European Act in 1986 (signed for the UK by Margaret Thatcher). Its specific aims were to create an 'internal market', an area without internal frontiers in which the free movement of goods, people, services and capital was ensured. The Single Market was perceived as presenting an opportunity for UK firms in continental Europe and DLC were active in market research on this. An internal study was undertaken for the DLE management board in 1990; DLC also undertook country studies between 1990 and 1991 for the Construction Industry Research and Information Association, the Royal Institute of British Architects and the Association of Consulting Engineers; and they produced a first edition of *Spon's European Price Book* in 1992. It is evident now that the potential for European crossborder work was exaggerated.

In fact, the main impact of the Single Market was to introduce a European regulatory framework within which the UK construction industry would be required to operate. The main elements of this were the Public Works Directive and a proposed Services Directive. The Public Works Directive has influenced both the way that quantity surveying firms get their work and the way in which 'public works' contracts are procured. All projects over a certain size have to be advertised in the *Official Journal of the European Union* and interested firms have to apply. This was complicated and time consuming and made access to public projects more uncertain for firms like DLE.

Cover of *Building* magazine, 7 May 1993.
Courtesy *Building*.

Partly prompted by efficiency reviews undertaken by the Conservative government, a Central Unit on Procurement (CUP) was set up in the Treasury in the early 1990s. This was staffed by a combination of civil servants and industry secondees and was the forerunner of what is now the Office of Government Commerce (OGC). CUP and OGC have both been involved in advising government departments and producing guidance on construction related matters. They have been influential on public procurement issues, particularly implementation of public private partnership projects and the establishment of framework agreements as a means of procuring services.

At the same time, the Property Services Agency (PSA), the central government client organisation, was finally broken up. The PSA had been put on a commercial footing in 1988 and in 1990 was split into Property Holdings, managing the government estate, and PSA Services, which bid for work from public sector, and other, organisations. In 1992, PSA Services was subdivided and sold off; PSA Projects, dealing with new projects, was purchased by Tarmac, the major contractor. The demise of the PSA ended central management of the government's building programme.

The Private Finance Initiative (PFI) was introduced in 1992 as a new procurement method designed to deliver public services by the private sector. In a construction-related PFI project, the private sector designs, builds, finances and operates an asset, a road, a hospital or a school, for example, and the user, the public sector agency, pays an annual user charge for a period of 25 or 30 years. It took time to design and refine the PFI process and the firm was involved, advising both users and service providers.

In 1993, Michael Latham was asked to undertake a wide ranging review of the construction industry.[6] An interim report, *Trust and Money,* was published in 1993 and his final report, *Constructing the Team,* the following year. Unlike previous reports on the industry, this was government supported but not government led; Latham's work was generally seen as independent, at least of government influence. The final report highlighted the role of the client in the construction process, the need for integrated supply chains and the need for new and collaborative forms of contract, addressing issues of payment and dispute resolution.

The report was well received by government but had a more mixed reception in the industry. Integrated supply chains threatened the position of both the professionals and the main contractors and emphasised the importance of specialist contractors (as both designers and constructors). The Latham Report, however, was a major event when it was published and still has influence on government and industry thinking. Insofar as reservations in the firm were expressed, they centred on the erosion of competition implied by integrated and collaborative working, how realistic giving a central role to clients was, and the practical difficulties of dealing with the concept of 'fairness' in construction contracts. Latham gave a presentation of his report to the assembled partners and staff of DLE and guests in Princes House in 1994.

The Latham Report also led to the establishment or reordering of industry bodies, including the creation of a Construction Industry Board (CIB), Construction Clients' Forum (CCF) and Constructors' Liaison Group (CLG), representing specialist contractors. The CIB became responsible for producing the codes of practice recommended by Latham and DLC was commissioned to prepare three of these.

In 1997, Sir John Egan was asked by the incoming Labour government to undertake another review of the industry. This was specifically directed to investigate how the processes and products of the construction industry could be improved and made more efficient. It also asked for best practice demonstration projects to be identified. The thinking behind this review was broadly similar to Latham's. The Egan task force largely consisted of clients of the industry, rather than consultants or contractors, although construction knowledge and expertise was drawn on from a variety of sources. The task force's report, *Rethinking Construction*, appeared in July 1998. The report's conclusions were not greatly different from Latham but they resulted in another industry body, the Movement for Innovation, and a key instrument for promoting the recommendations, demonstration projects. Like Latham, they were better accepted by government than by the industry.

Both Latham and Egan, but particularly the latter, were critical of the UK construction industry; it was seen as fragmented, inefficient and confrontational. It is difficult to see exactly how the two reports have improved the industry but clearly their existence, including their preparation and their aftermath stimulated much discussion and some analysis of the industry and some of that will have been helpful. Within a few years, however, many of the bodies brought into being by Latham and Egan had collapsed or been replaced and the codes of practice have not become mainstream industry documents. The adoption by government of the Latham and Egan analyses and prescriptions has probably not been particularly helpful.

Finally, private clients, particularly the leading developers, encouraged and sometimes initiated different procurement and contractual arrangements for their projects, usually designed for 'fast-track' management-type projects.

These, and the innovations introduced and changes made, by government and the European Union, led to a greater involvement of project managers and lawyers in the construction process. The old certainties, and possibly inefficiencies, of standard building contracts, processes and procedures were ended.

Stanhope, the developers, and Stuart Lipton, their chairman, deserve special mention as innovators in both the development process and its product and as a major influence on Davis Langdon and its approach. Starting in the early 1980s in a series of projects including Cutlers Court, No. 1 Finsbury Square, Broadgate and Stockley Park, they transformed the London commercial property market. Davis Langdon first worked with Stanhope on Building B2 at Stockley Park with Troughton McAslan. The relationship was highly influential, particularly with a group of younger partners led by Paul Morrell and that influence is still evident in the firm's workload and approach.

Internal Changes

The internal changes stimulated by the merger flowed from the detailed understanding of both firms revealed by the pre-merger due diligence exercises and the need to work out in some detail a new organisation for the merged firm, replacing the more precedent based, unwritten rules of the old partnerships. Principal changes were the establishment of a more formal structure for the business and initial moves to a more national practice.

At the time of the merger two changes were made to branch partner arrangements. The local office share was increased by ten per cent and all offices, including London, were required to allocate 20 per cent of their profits to a central 'pot' which was then distributed to offices in line with their profitability over the previous three years.

In October 1991 there was a major debate at the annual partners' conference on the financial structure of the firm, including profit sharing, the share of the London office in branches and the senior partners' remuneration. Two main models of profit sharing were discussed: a greater pooling and sharing of profits and largely maintaining the status quo whereby local income was primarily tied to local performance but with the introduction of minimum incomes. The debate ended with around half of the partnership in favour of a single pool but a two thirds majority was required so the old model was retained.

Shortly afterwards, the London partners' share was discussed and resolved. Historically, branch offices were established as joint ventures between the

London partners and a local partner hence the London partners had an interest in all offices but local partners only had an interest in their office. In return, London provided some central services. It was agreed that the branch partners would buy out the London partners' share over a ten year period from future profits. Linked to the abandonment of the London partners' share was an agreement that branches would contribute to central services and that there would be more management board oversight of individual offices' performance.

Although the wider profit sharing arrangement was not resolved, agreement on minimum incomes, the London share and the remuneration of the senior partner were achievements. But the issue of profit sharing in a national practice had been raised and would return regularly over the coming years.

Following the structure debate, the firm appointed an individual who was to become an important agent of change in their moves towards more professional management, stricter financial control and a more corporate style. In 1992, Jeremy Horner was appointed as finance partner, replacing the company secretary, Stuart Greenstreet, who retired. He was a chartered accountant with a background in investment banking and within a couple of years was to become the first non-construction professional equity partner in the business. This was the first in what is now an established cadre of senior management with functional rather than fee-earning roles. Although it was a conscious decision of the partners, or at least the management board, to start along this route, Horner has been a consistent advocate and facilitator of the approach. DLE was not the first QS firm to take the corporate route but has been successful in combining a traditional partnership (now a Limited Liability Partnership) with corporate structure and management.

The emergence of modern human resources management from the more traditional personnel function introduced a number of new ideas, including staff, and later partner, reviews, staff and management development programmes, graduate training, annual staff days, and an in-house magazine. Prior to the merger, responsibility for personnel matters was shared between administrative staff and the partners and its scope was limited to staff conditions; from 1988 there was a dedicated functional HR manager and a growing team of HR professionals.

In a competitive environment, marketing and public relations became ever more important. The merger itself was recognised at the time as a great marketing opportunity and was well exploited as one. Alastair Collins was taken out of his role as a project partner and appointed the firm's first Business Development partner. A new Business Development department

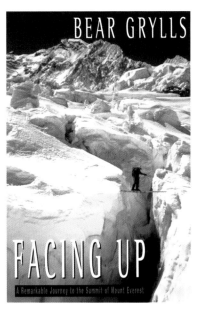

took on a whole range of tasks, previously undertaken by individual partners or not done at all, including the preparation of brochures for sectors and services, prequalification registrations, scanning job opportunities, for example in the *Official Journal of the EU*, compilation of presentation material and organisation of presentation training and the organisation of the firm's participation in events.

In the 1990s, the tradition of Davis Langdon Summer Receptions was established, sometimes taking advantage of recently completed DLE projects. There were receptions for clients and colleagues at the British Library and Somerset House, for example. The idea of Davis Langdon Sponsorship also emerged in the 1990s with support for a solo trans-Atlantic sailing race from Quebec to St Malo with Nic Bailey, an ex-Fosters man, but a more impressive and appropriate opportunity was to appear completely serendipitously.

In February 1998, a young man cycling up Kingsway saw the name Davis Langdon & Everest on the entrance canopy to No 39, Princes House. It was Bear Grylls who, at the time, was urgently seeking sponsorship for his lifetime's ambition, climbing Mount Everest. He left a brochure with the receptionist and asked that it be passed to the senior partner. Two days later he received a phone call asking him to come in for a conversation. He was interviewed by Nick Davis, outgoing senior partner, Paul Morrell, incoming senior partner, and Collins and, after he had outlined his plans, he was told that he was just what they were looking for: something to excite the whole firm. At the end of the meeting, Grylls had his main sponsor. Two weeks later he set off for Everest and was interviewed at base camp via satellite phone by Rob Smith, the London managing partner at a London staff day. In May 1998 he became the (then) youngest British climber to conquer Everest.[7] When he returned to the UK, Grylls undertook a series of talks for the firm's staff, clients and friends.

In its first ten years, DLE achieved impressive press coverage for a firm of quantity surveyors. There were regular awards and regular articles in *Building* and the *AJ* and the firms' projects were regularly featured in the technical press. While the senior partners of the firm all received the accolade of a front cover in *Building*, another partner achieved another, more design-orientated, kind of recognition. An interview with Clyde Malby appeared in *World Architecture* in September 1992 under the title, "God's Own QS" with his photograph alongside.

Also in the early 1990s, clients began to insist on formal prequalification requirements for their consultants. With the abandonment of scale fees and

Top: The cover of Bear Grylls' book *Facing Up*, published by Pan Macmillan, 2000.
© Bear Grylls 2000.

Bottom: Clyde Malby, September 1992.
Courtesy *World Architecture*.

the introduction of competition, clients wanted to be able to filter the firms who sought to work for them. This was particularly the case in the public sector where departments, authorities and agencies were not only required to select on the basis of competition but also had to demonstrate value for money and satisfy public accountability requirements. One of the first and more bureaucratically demanding requirements was Quality Assurance (QA).

Good professional firms have always had procedures to ensure that the right things were done at the right time in the right order, but these often did not include formal sign-offs and mandatory use. The better firms had comprehensive office procedure manuals and guidelines but these were not necessarily rigorously enforced. QA required a formal set of procedures for everything the firm did on projects and these needed to be signed off by an authorised certification authority and the firm was subject to regular audits. The result was QA certification and Davis Langdon & Everest secured that for QS services in London in 1992. Other offices and services followed.

Investors In People (IIP) was also embarked on as a London office initiative but not till later in the decade.[8] IIP specifically recognised the importance of a firm's people; its scope included clarifying the firm's vision and purpose and ensuring best practice in the recruitment, development, remuneration and evaluation of everyone in the firm. Like QA, it required the firm to do many of the things it already did but in a more structured and consistent way and, like QA, it needed independent accreditation. A principal aim was to involve staff more in the operation of the business. Regular reviews were introduced to provide a formal opportunity for staff and managers to talk to each other and share objectives and concerns. And final business planning processes were required setting out what the partners intended and helping identify where everyone's contributions fitted in. The London office was accredited as IIP in 1998.

Project Management

Project management as a distinct service in UK construction emerged in the 1970s, partly from other sectors and other countries; and partly in response to the increasing complexity of some projects and a disinclination by some designers to manage them. Pressure on revenue and profits from the removal of mandatory scale fees and more overt competition for work may also have encouraged development of a new service, some of which was already being provided by some firms. Sectoral origins for project management included process and industrial engineering; international origins were most frequently from the USA but often first experienced by UK firms in the Middle East.[9]

Top left: Bank of England,
Sheppard Robson/epr.
Top right: Somerset House, London,
for the Somerset Trust. Gilbert Collection, South
Wing, Somerset House, London: Peter Inskip &
Peter Jenkins.
Centre left: Royal Academy of Music, London,
John McAslan & Partners.
Courtesy Peter Cook/View.
Centre right: The Eden Project, St Austell,
Cornwall, Nicholas Grimshaw & Partners.
Bottom: Serpentine Gallery, Hyde Park, London,
John Miller & Partners.

Derek Johnson.

Unlike some of their competitors, both DB&E and L&E avoided establishing separate project management units for most of the 1980s.[10] They were busy enough and, certainly in the case of DB&E, thought that it could upset relations with clients and designers. They both, however, undertook some management work. Tim Carter, originally based in the Chester office of DB&E, was an early proponent of project management and worked on major projects from the 1970s, including the Bank of America Computer Centre in Croydon. From 1992 to 1996 he worked on No. 1 Poultry in the City of London, designed by James Stirling and, from 1996 to 2003, on the job that was to cap his career, the Eden Project in Cornwall, designed by Nicholas Grimshaw & Partners.

Other parts of the firm also effectively operated as managers including L&E's work for Bupa in the early 1980s. Their role was much more extensive than traditional quantity surveying and included selection and appointment of designers; it was project management in all but name.

Shortly after the merger, the management board decided to develop a dedicated project management capability in London. Derek Johnson had joined DB&E in 1987, initially as a freelance, Davis Langdon Management (DLM) was formed in 1989 and Johnson became a partner in the following year. In parallel with developing DLM, Johnson undertook the Masters course in Project Management at Reading University (1987–1990). Although he was based in London, the DLM brand was also used by other offices, including Chester, where Tim Carter was based. Projects initially came from referrals from quantity surveying partners but work was also secured independently.

In the mid-1990s a number of Millennium Arts and Heritage commissions were won, including the Eden Project and Galleries at Somerset House for the Gilbert Collection. There were projects at the National Gallery, Royal Academy of Music and Royal Academy of Arts. They also undertook projects for the Bank of England, theatre refurbishments and social housing. DLM had a mixed portfolio, mostly (around 70 per cent) with DLE as quantity surveyors and mostly for one-off or less experienced clients.

In 1998 a decision was made to organise the London office as integrated project and cost management teams, that is, to distribute project managers across the cost management teams. The plan was to offer an integrated service. This model was operated for five years but in 2003 a dedicated project management team was recreated under Johnson and a new partner, John Lewis. At that time, there were less than 50 project managers in London although there was an increasing number of project managers in offices around the country. In 1990, fee income was £450,000, representing one per cent of turnover, in

2003 it was around 6 million pounds and 17 per cent of turnover and total staff nationally was around 70. It has been consistently successful in receiving industry recognition and awards.

From the beginning, there were different views about DLE providing Project Management both inside and outside the firm. Many, if not all, partners saw it as an essential development of the firm's repertoire of services but others were concerned that some designers they worked with would be concerned about the firm taking on a management role on projects. Some clients liked the idea of a joint service but it was anathema to others. In fact, it was a natural progression for a firm like DLE and is now looked upon as a core service.

Growth through Mergers

By the end of Nick Davis' tenure in 1998, workload had recovered and there was an air of optimism in the business that had not been there for five years. His successor, Paul Morrell, was appointed after a partnership election (the other candidate was Rob Smith, who was to succeed Morrell). He was 51 and had been a partner since 1976. Like his predecessors, he was granted a front cover of *Building*. Morrell was very clear about his aspirations: he wanted clearer and better national and international structures; he wanted a corporate strategy and a business plan; he wanted value adding processes and products; and he wanted the best people.

Both L&E and DB&E had grown organically. Prior to the late 1990s there had been only a very few joint-ventures, mergers or take-overs. In the early 1990s there were a series of joint-venture companies in continental Europe, most of which had unravelled or stagnated by the late 1990s; in 1989, Oxford and East Anglia Regional Heath Authority quantity surveyors were taken over and subsumed in the DLE Oxford and Cambridge offices when the technical services of the authorities were privatised; there was a merger with Clarence Smart & Partners, quantity surveyors, in Peterborough; and a small firm, Ray May & Associates, joined DLE in the mid-1990s.

Morrell had decided that growth in both scope and scale was essential but it was evident to him that expansion, and particularly planned expansion, was difficult to achieve organically. The response was a more proactive approach to growth. In three years, between 1999 and 2002, a series of ten mergers (see the table on page 135) were completed in different locations and for different reasons.

There were three basic rationales: to reinforce core cost management resources in a particular location; to add a new, or supplement an existing specialist, service; and to expand the firm internationally. Needless to say these sometimes overlapped; some target locations had a range of service offerings and sometimes a service existed in more than one location. The basic philosophy adopted was that the mergers should not be purchases of businesses and that the principals of target firms would become principals of Davis Langdon, although not necessarily equity partners. The intention was always to maintain the existing business and incorporate it into Davis Langdon's business.

UK Mergers

Leighton & Wright

The merger with Leighton & Wright in South Wales was primarily to support Paul Edwards, then a sole partner in Cardiff. Jim Leighton and Steve Wright had been with Symonds and had set up on their own as quantity surveyors in 1998. Shortly after the merger with DLE, Wright left the partnership and since then DLE's work in Wales has been led by Edwards and Leighton.

Poole Stokes & Wood

The merger with Poole Stokes & Wood (PSW) was initiated by Paul Stanion of PSW and Andrew Thomson, the Manchester partner of DLE. They knew each other well, had common clients and got on. The merger created the largest firm of quantity surveyors in the North-West and helped resolve leadership issues in the region. PSW had offices in Manchester, Birmingham and London. Manchester was the main office and was successful, as a consultant to Manchester City Council, particularly on sports buildings and social housing.

Birmingham was locationally attractive, DLE was keen to have an office in the city. The PSW office needed major reorganisation and indirectly that led to Birmingham becoming the support service centre of the firm. The London office of PSW was 15 strong and the two partners and staff were taken into the London office. Alan Willby, one of the partners, rapidly built on his sports expertise and is, most recently, resident partner on the 2012 Olympics development.

Mott Green & Wall

The next merger was with London based quantity surveyors, Mott Green & Wall (MGW). MGW was the premier firm of specialised quantity surveyors for mechanical and electrical engineering (M&E) work, that often represented more than a third of a project's value. The founding partners had gone and the firm, now a company, was led by second generation directors, Ken Chesshire and Barry Nugent.[11]

DB&E and L&E, like most major QS firms, had both worked hard since the 1960s at developing a sound M&E capability and, post-merger, they had maintained that.[12] Over the years, they had tried separate M&E departments and integrating M&E into QS teams, always headed by a quantity surveyor. What they did not achieve, however, was the reputation of being the best M&E quantity surveyor; that was the attraction of MGW.

DLE and MGW were working together on a number of commercial developments in the late 1990s. The prospect of a merger was broached by Rob Smith in a conversation with Barry Nugent of MGW in 1998 but, after some initial exchanges, it was dropped, amicably. MGW had been courted by a number of the major firms and these kind of approaches were nothing new. Nine months later Smith again approached Nugent and suggested they try again. They did, involving Paul Morrell, and within a few months terms were agreed. A key element for Chesshire and Nugent, the joint managing directors, was that the MGW name was retained.

MGW were Stanhope's preferred M&E surveyors and Stanhope, apparently, had mixed feelings about the merger. Stanhope was and is a major commercial developer and commercial development manager. On the one hand they liked the idea of two of their favourite firms getting together; but, on the other, they liked the independent advice they got from both firms. This was not an uncommon response from clients but the nett result of the merger was to increase both firms' business and to satisfy most of their clients.

Schumann Smith
In 1999 Nick Schumann was talking to Paul Morrell at a House of Commons cocktail party and commented that they would work well together. They both knew each other, not least through work over many years with Norman Foster's practice. Morrell was preoccupied with the PSW and MGW mergers but when they were concluded he thought about the Schumann Smith approach. There was some concern that they were close to architects when the more recent instinct of DLE was to be close to clients. On the other hand, like MGW, they were 'best in class'. Nick Schumann and Rob Smith talked and the concerns were allayed with the result that the firms merged in May 2000.

NBW Crosher & James
Paul Morrell had an idea of DLE as a construction based management consultancy and a key element of that was financial and taxation consultancy. The firm had a small group working on capital allowances and construction VAT but it was not the best or the best known. That was NBW Crosher & James, originally a QS practice that dated back to the 1930s but which, since

the 1980s, had concentrated on construction taxation and had become 'the' specialist firm competing directly, and successfully, with the big accountancy firms. Jimmy James, the son of one of the founders, had effectively invented construction related taxation advice.

The merger was initiated by Richard Pitman, a DLE partner in the Southampton office. Locally, the two firms had agreed to work together. Meetings were arranged with senior representatives of both firms and the merger was completed in 2001.

Stockings & Clark

Stockings & Clark was a quantity surveying firm in Norwich with a particular focus on the food industry. Most merger discussions were held locally but with the approval of the management board, and Stockings & Clark was taken into the East Anglia Region in 2001.

International Mergers

The international mergers in this period were different in nature to the UK mergers. The *verein* was used in 1999 as the vehicle for the international 'holding company', Davis Langdon & Seah International (DLSI) (see "Chapter Six"). This left ownership and profit with each member of the *verein* and focused on common standards, marketing and research. The model was one adopted by a number of the large international accountancy and legal firms. Advantages were that it took money, with all the associated problems, out of the relationship. And that made international agreement easier. The disadvantages related to the 'looseness' of the relationship.

The four associations, in South Africa, the USA, New Zealand and the Republic of Ireland all consolidated existing relationships and, because of the *verein*, were relatively easy to negotiate and agree. They have all also been successful.

Farrow Laing

There had been links with Farrow Laing in the 1960s and possibly earlier but there had been no joint projects and the days of the apartheid regime in South Africa had made close links impractical. With the release from prison of Nelson Mandela and the progressive moves towards full democracy and the end of apartheid, the barriers to public and closer association were removed. Alastair Collins, a former partner of Farrow Laing, who had been based in the UK for some time, joined Davis Langdon in 1990 and helped to re-establish contacts.

Original Name of Firm	Locations	Date of Merger	Notes
National			
Leighton & Wright	South Wales	1999	Quantity surveyors
Poole Stokes & Wood	Manchester Birmingham London	1999	Established 1965; joined DLE in 1999. Quantity surveyors
Mott Green & Wall	London	1999	Established 1970; joined DLE as Davis Langdon Mott Green Wall in 1999. Mechanical and Electrical Services Quantity surveyors
Schumann Smith	Stevenage	2000	Established 1986; joined DLE as Davis Langdon Schumann Smith in 2000. Specification consultants
NBW Crosher & James	London Birmingham Glasgow Edinburgh	2001	Crosher & James established 1935, Napier Blakely Winter was established 1988, NBW C&J established 2000; joined DLE as Davis Langdon Crosher & James in 2001. Construction Taxation consultants
Stockings & Clark	East Anglia	2001	Quantity surveyors
International			
Farrow Laing & Partners	South Africa	1999	Established 1922; joined DLSI in 1999; became Davis Langdon Africa in 2004. Quantity surveyors
Adamson Associates	USA	1999	Established 1974; joined DLSI in 1999 as Davis Langdon Adamson in 2006. Cost consultants
Knapman Clark & Co	New Zealand	1999	Established 1954; joined DLSI in 1999 as Davis Langdon Knapman Clark; became Davis Langdon New Zealand in 2000. Quantity surveyors
Patterson Kempster & Shortall	Republic of Ireland	2002	Established 1860; joined DLSI in 2002 as Davis Langdon PKS. Quantity surveyors

Table showing UK and International mergers, 1999–2002.

There were staff and work exchanges, mainly South African staff coming to the UK and, later in the decade, work being outsourced from the UK to South Africa as the UK market recovered and grew. In 1999 after much discussion, the partners of Farrow Laing joined the DLSI *verein* as Davis Langdon Farrow Laing.

Adamson Associates

Links with Adamson Associates had been established in the early 1990s and after working together it was relatively easy to suggest a closer relationship. Paul Morrell, senior partner of Davis Langdon, and Martin Gordon, chairman of Adamsons, agreed to join forces formally and Adamson Associates joined the *verein* as Davis Langdon Adamson the same year as Farrow Laing.

Knapman Clark

Knapman Clark in New Zealand also joined the *verein* in 1999. The initial links were via the Australian part of DLSI and when these became more formalised the New Zealanders were invited to become part of DLSI. The Knapman Clark suffix was dropped in 2000.

Patterson Kempster & Shortall (PKS)

Links with PKS went back many years and there were a number of close personal relations among partners, exchanges of personnel and joint projects. As with the other international mergers, any reluctance was more to do with concerns over real or apparent loss of national independence. DLSI's *verein* structure allowed the national practices to join an international group rather than be taken over by a UK firm. PKS became part of DLSI in 2002.

New Offices

The partners in London had made a step change when they moved to Princes House in 1990. It was a modern professional working environment attractive to both staff and clients. But the same could not be said about most of the regional offices. With few exceptions, they were generally undistinguished in both location and appearance.

When Paul Morrell became senior partner in 1998, he embarked on a campaign of exposing the worst offenders. A natural performer, Morrell, in his regular presentations to partners, delighted in showing the most unattractive views of the firm's regional offices to their peers. During his tenure, a number of them were upgraded or replaced. Again, the impact on staff and clients was immeasurable, although there were the inevitable 'old timers' who saw no need for change.

The Structure Debate Revisited

The partner remuneration system developed in the early 1990s combined grouping offices into regions and sharing profit locally and in a central profit pool. The end result was that the vast majority of an individual partner's income depended on their region's financial performance. It did not encourage partners to do anything that did not secure fee income for their region or to move to another region or office unless it was more profitable. It encouraged partners in different regions to compete for work and clients and dissuaded them from collaborating. On the other hand, the system kept partners motivated, there was a very direct financial connection between what they did and the income they received.

Partner profit share progression within an office or a region moved in a pre-arranged pattern to a plateau level and could create discontent. Some partners believed that they were undercompensated and that other partners were over compensated. A significant proportion of, if not all, partners recognised that the system was flawed but there were different views on how it should be resolved. The situation was also complicated by the partners all being quantity surveyors, highly numerate and ever willing to develop highly complex systems.

Davis Langdon office at
40 Princes Street, Edinburgh.

Although the move from single offices to regions was generally beneficial, as the firm became larger, the number of local projects and clients declined and

the number of national projects and clients increased. The issues, therefore, were: should compensation be based more on individual, local, regional or national success; should progression within the partnership be automatic or based on some kind of performance assessment; and, in any case, was financial performance the only real measure of individual or group value.

In 2000, the system was changed to a national pool coupled with formal Partner Development Reviews (PDRs). The latter was designed to assess a range of partners' contributions to the business, not only their financial contribution. These included bringing in clients and work, delivering projects, managing clients, developing people, cross-referring work and promoting the firm. Despite all their best efforts, however, the tendency was for financial performance to over-ride other factors. In addition, the national pool and individual reviews were viewed as undermining the strength of the regions; geography continued to dominate allocation of the profit pool.

Commentary

1990 to 2003 saw the transformation of Davis Langdon & Everest from a large firm of quantity surveyors into a major international construction professional services firm. In 1990, the newly merged firm was two years

Davis Langdon Birmingham office,
Colmore Plaza.

old and still under the joint senior partnership of Mike McLeod and Geoff Trickey. The move of staff from the two old firms' London offices to a new office at Princes House in Kingsway went ahead that year with the old L&E staff moving in January and the old DB&E people in July.

The industry changed dramatically from 1989 to 1993, that is, from just before the recession started until the beginning of the recovery. Trends that had been beginning to be evident in the late 1980s became dominant features of the industry landscape five years later. Just as the industry was changing, so was the firm. The merger had happened but co-location in London did not arrive until 1990. During the early 1990s much was done to bring the two firms and their ways of working together and to tweak the systems devised at the time of the merger.

The mergers in the three years from 1999 were remarkable in enabling Davis Langdon to grow and diversify both in the UK and internationally, through DLSI. They brought people, skills and contacts that were among the best in the business. Like the 1988 merger of DB&E and L&E, they were undertaken in a buoyant UK construction market and, like that merger, have all been successful.

QA and IIP were important because they required the involvement of virtually everyone in the firm. It was no longer possible to manage the firm in a top down way, however benevolently. By the end of the 1990s, DLE was a modern firm in modern offices with formally accredited procedures, although really only in London. But the case was made internally and by the early years of the new century, the firm throughout the UK was consistent in its standards and procedures.

Information and communications technology was to provide another kind of glue, although it took time and expense and some frustration before the firm was to be fully and reliably wired. To move from 20 desktop PCs in London in 1990 to a fully networked national system ten years later called for major investment, faith and vision.

Fee competition was now 'normal', particularly for public sector clients. Even with long term private sector clients, although formal fee bidding was often not required, informal market testing was expected. That is, client and consultant discussed and agreed appropriate fee rates in the light of prevailing market conditions.

Unsurprisingly, tender prices plummeted with the collapse in construction orders. The graph overleaf shows the collapse in all new orders and the DLE tender price index from 1986 to 1995.

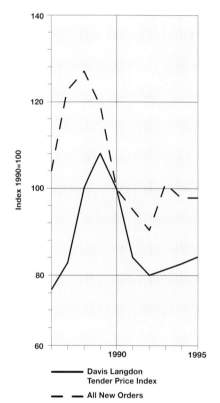

140

120

Index 1990=100

100

80

60

1990   1995

——— Davis Langdon
Tender Price Index

— — All New Orders

Graph showing all new orders and the Davis
Langdon Tender Price Index, 1986 to 1995.
Source: Office for National Statistics (ONS)
and Davis Langdon.

After their peaks in 1988 and 1989 orders and prices did not recover 1987 levels for a number of years. Not only, therefore, did workload decline but, as a result of competition, *ad valorem* fee percentages reduced and so did the contract prices on which they were being charged, a triple whammy!

One of the results of all the initiatives and pressures, internal and external, was a fundamental change in what the firm did and what its outputs were. By the late 1990s Davis Langdon produced relatively few bills of quantities, the traditional output of quantity surveying firms. It now largely provided construction cost advice and produced pricing documents for contractors that varied in form from specifications of works to cost plans. These were not compiled in accordance with a standard method of measurement and had differing contractual status.

Other changes that had started in the 1980s and accelerated in the 1990s were in the relative importance of the main participants in the construction process. These included declines in the leadership roles of public clients and architects and increases in the roles and responsibilities of main and sub-contractors and construction and project managers. Davis Langdon had traditionally aligned themselves with architects and public sector or owner occupier clients and had a general 'contractor rule' whereby the firm did not work for contractors.

In the late 1980s, the firm's emerging focus was on clients of all types but particularly private commercial clients. Partners and staff remained supportive of architects and architecture but recognised their reduced importance. Procurement models like PFI and PPP placed contractors in the role of clients as well as contractors and made the contractor rule increasingly difficult to enforce. Contractors and consultant project managers were frequently initiators and leaders of projects; they were quasi-clients and could not be ignored. And the firm, itself, was beginning to be a force in project management.

Davis Langdon had also diversified its range of services over the period. In addition to the 17 per cent of revenues from project management in 2003, a further ten per cent was contributed by other services including legal, taxation, specification and management consultancy. A firm that was primarily quantity surveyors in 1990, not much more than a decade later earned almost 30 per cent of its income from 'other services'.

The firm had also modernised and restructured its internal operations and its working environment. It had moved away from a traditional partnership to a much more corporate structure with full time functional heads for finance,

IT and HR. The firm was run by a relatively small management board elected by the partners and a series of partnership changes had been introduced, primarily to break down internal competition between offices. Formal business planning had been introduced and attitudes towards that and other changes had moved from initial suspicion through acceptance to active participation. Internal communications of all kinds had improved and regular staff and partner reviews were commonplace.

The period from 1993 to 2003 was one of growth and change in the construction sector, slow at first but gathering pace. By a combination of luck and good judgement, DLE was able to join in the growth and at the end of the period was both larger and stronger than it had ever been.

1   The graph can be compared to those on page 38 (1955–1970) and page 57 (1970–1990). All three are compiled on the same basis and drawn to the same scale.

2   Private housing and private commercial orders were 63 per cent of all new orders in 2006, a probable indicator of overheating.

3   Mandatory fee scales were withdrawn in 1984 but boom conditions had largely sheltered firms, particularly in the South-East, from its extreme effects.

4   The DLE tender price index peaked in 1989, fell by 50 per cent to 1993 then doubled from 1993 to 2000 (back to 1989 levels).

5   The report was published as *QS2000, The Future Role of the Quantity Surveyor* in June 1991. Interestingly, it was the last such report published by the RICS.

6   Latham was a Conservative MP who had some experience and understanding of construction, he had been a housing advisor in both Labour and Conservative administrations and a director of the House Builders Federation.

7   The story is told in Gryll's book, *Facing Up*, published by Macmillan in 2000.

8   IIP is a UK government Non-departmental Public Body established in 1994. Its purpose is to support organisations in developing and looking after their people.

9   Early US practitioners in the UK include Schal and Heery.

10 Gardiner & Theobald, for example, established Gardiner & Theobald Management Services (GTMS) in the early 1980s.

11 Chesshire died suddenly in 2002.

12 Derek Mott and Peter Green, two of the founders of MGW, had worked with DB&E in the 1960s.

Chapter Eight

Not Just a Quantity Surveyor

In 1988, both Langdon & Every (L&E) and Davis Belfield & Everest (DB&E) were largely traditional firms of quantity surveyors in terms of the work they did and the way they did it. By far the greatest source of income in both cases was from the provision of quantity surveying services. And quantity surveying was, by and large, a well-defined process with comprehensive and standardised rules, not least the Standard Method of Measurement (SMM), a familiar set of services and a standard product, the bill of quantities. That is not to say that the firms did not provide other services or advice but that they were generally not sold separately; it was assumed by clients and others that the major firms, and in particular their senior staff and partners, were able to comment and advise in an informed way on a range of activities related to construction and property.

A trend towards diversification by quantity surveyors had begun in the 1970s and accelerated in the 1980s. The initial prompts for DLE were client demand, the personal interests of particular individuals in the firm and, by the late 1980s, a belief in the partnership that some diversification was necessary. Geoff Trickey recalls being pressed by a major retail client to take on project management responsibilities for a major job and reluctantly having to decline. Another rationale, particularly after the recession in the early 1990s, was to generate additional revenue-earning activities as fees for traditional services came under increasing competitive pressures. Services that were provided 'free of charge' under RICS full scale fees began to become 'additional services'.

The current set of Specialist Services in Davis Langdon comprises: Banking, Tax and Finance; Building Surveying; CDM Consultancy; Engineering Services; Legal Support Services; Management Consulting; Specification and Design Management; and Value, Planning and Risk Management. These have all become distinct operational units although they were not always so and there are sometimes overlaps among them and between them and the core Cost and Project Management services.

Banking, Tax and Finance

The firm and its predecessors have always advised on tax issues as they affected construction; Colin Brearley, for example, advised Great Portland Estates on VAT matters in the 1970s. Construction taxation as a distinct service in Davis Langdon started with Peter Cummings, an associate based in the Legal Support team, in the early 1990s. The location in the Legal Support team was not because they were similar but, rather, because both were different from the core service.

A number of quantity surveying firms had begun to provide services in construction-related capital allowances and VAT in the 1970s.[1] Their development followed the increase in the volume and complexity of legislation through the 1970s and 1980s and was paralleled in a number of accountancy firms. When Cummings left in the mid-1990s to join one of the major firms of accountants, Andy White and Julian Potts were recruited from Gleeds. Construction Taxation became a distinct but small service line and separate profit centre in Davis Langdon in 2001.

In mid-2000, a small group of NBW Crosher & James partners were invited to lunch by four partners of Davis Langdon, hosted by Paul Morrell, senior partner. Half an hour into lunch Tony Llewellyn of Croshers asked Morrell why they had been invited to lunch. Morrell asked if they would be interested in merging with Davis Langdon. It took about four months of discussion and negotiation; heads of agreement were drafted by January 2001 and the merger was finalised on 1 May 2001. The result was a specialist business unit called Davis Langdon Crosher & James.

NBW Crosher & James was the result of a merger in 2000 between Napier Blakely & Winter (established 1988) and Crosher & James (established 1935). Interestingly, Napier, Blakely and Winter were all ex-Crosher & James people. At the time of the merger with Davis Langdon, Croshers had nine partners, 33 staff and offices in London, Birmingham, Glasgow and Edinburgh.

Bill James was born in 1913 and began his career, aged 17, articled to F&HF Higgs. In 1933, he joined Gardiner & Theobald and there met his future partners, father and son, William and Wilfrid Crosher. The firm of Crosher & James was founded in 1935. William (Bill) Crosher was 36 years older than James, he had worked as a civil servant in various ministries and had good public sector connections. Wilfrid Crosher was a similar age to James. In their early days a major client was the Air Ministry, in preparation for the Second World War. The work they did was traditional quantity surveying.

Not much is known about the firm of Crosher & James before, during and immediately after the Second World War but we do know that relations between Bill Crosher and Bill James were strained and the origins of that were in the division of profits. The two only communicated in writing from shortly after the partnership was formed and, as a result, James worked hard to develop his own clients and his own workload. His focus was on private commercial clients in contrast to Crosher's public sector connections. Crosher senior died in 1955 at the age of 78.

James joined the Quantity Surveyors' committee of the Royal Institution of Chartered Surveyors in the early 1940s and from then on he was rarely without a role in the Institution. Partly as a result of this, he built up strong connections with City institutions and long term clients of Crosher & James included insurance companies such as Sun Alliance, Cornhill and Guardian. His son, Jimmy, joined the firm as a partner in the late 1960s and opened an office in the Midlands, in Solihull, working for British Leyland and Midlands property developers. After a few busy years the firm's workload came to a sudden halt with the 1973 property crash. As a result, Jimmy went off to work overseas, in Beirut but left there hastily in the mid-1970s when the Lebanese Civil War became too dangerous. On his return to the UK he started talking to property clients about the potential savings from the application of capital allowances, something he had begun to develop an interest in the early 1970s.

James became a specialist in the analysis and interpretation of tax legislation as it applied to property and in the early days often had to explain aspects of the legislation not only to his clients but also to the tax authorities. In addition to advice on capital allowances, James developed leasing contracts and other innovative financial arrangements.

Crosher & James continued as a firm of quantity surveyors through the 1980s and 1990s with tax related services representing an increasing proportion of the firm's workload and income. At the time of the merger with Davis Langdon, they were the largest and best known firm of specialist tax advisers on property and construction. The business model was very different from the Davis Langdon core service. It involved 'cold calling'; fee income comprised a large number of relatively small fees (£5,000 was a typical Crosher & James job fee); but the value of the service was evident and direct. It was possible to identify exactly the saving that had resulted from Crosher & James' advice.

In recent years, more services have been added to the tax group's repertoire, including advice on project funding, grants and loans, due diligence and banking advisory services. The services bridge the worlds of construction, property and finance and are aimed at providing reassurance to the funders of projects who are often not construction experts. The group also regularly publishes information and guidance notes on different aspects of their services.

From 42 strong, including partners, at the time of the merger, the Banking Tax and Finance Group numbered some 80 people and had an annual turnover of £9 million in 2008. Partners and staff are located in nine offices across the UK and there is an international outpost in Johannesburg, South Africa. Tony Llewellyn, former senior partner of NBW Crosher & James is on the Executive of Davis Langdon in his capacity as head of Specialist Services.

Tony Llewellyn, former Head of new Crosher & James, currently Head of Specialist Services.

Building Surveying

Like many firms of quantity surveyors, Davis Langdon has always employed building surveyors and at least one of the early partners, Colin Brearley, qualified as a chartered building surveyor. It was always useful to have someone in the office who could produce drawings and specifications and was familiar with issues like dilapidations and party-wall agreements. Largely unconsciously, during the 1990s and the early years of the new century, Davis Langdon acquired an increasing number of building surveyors through mergers with mainly quantity surveying firms in the regions.

In 2007, when the merger with Mackenzies in Scotland was being discussed, Gordon Stirling, their Building Surveying partner, asked Sam Mackenzie of Davis Langdon how many building surveyors the firm employed. Mackenzie's initial response was "two or three" but he promised to check and establish a more accurate figure. The correct answer was actually somewhere nearer to 35 but mostly located as individuals or two or three people in separate offices and with no organised national service coordination or leadership.

In Mackenzies, Stirling had under him an 18 strong group across the Scottish offices and the building surveying fee income represented some 25 per cent of the firm's total income. There was clearly the beginnings of a new Davis Langdon service and, in 2008, Stirling was appointed as its head and set about combining the disparate resources in the firm. There are now a total of 70 building surveyors in eight offices, with Glasgow, Liverpool and Birmingham having the largest complements.[2] The national turnover is around £6 million. Services typically include large-scale condition surveys, long-term maintenance plans, the management of maintenance and refurbishment projects, disability access audits and, more recently, the preparation of Energy Performance Certificates (EPCs). There is a slight tension related to the provision of building surveying in that the service can get close to 'design' and offering design services is something that the firm has consistently and studiously avoided.

CDM Consultancy

The Construction (Design and Management), the CDM Regulations were introduced in 1994 in order to implement key aspects of a European Directive. They identified the need to address health and safety risks on building sites and placed explicit responsibilities on building clients and designers. Despite their importance and legal force, effective take-up was relatively slow. Over the past few years, the Health and Safety Executive has worked hard to raise awareness and new regulations, CDM 2007, were introduced in 2007.

Nationally, there are 18 planning supervisors in Davis Langdon, all qualified Health and Safety professionals, under John Allcock, partner in Milton Keynes. Half of the staff are based in Milton Keynes, others are in Peterborough, Birmingham and Scotland. More than half the team's turnover of £2 million is earned on Davis Langdon projects, the remainder on direct appointments.

Engineering Services

Mechanical and electrical (M&E) services in buildings, plumbing, heating, lifts, air conditioning, and other installations, have become progressively more complex and more expensive, over the past few decades. Their contribution to the total costs of building has probably increased from around 25 per cent to, say, 40 per cent since the 1950s. Traditional quantity surveying and surveyors did not deal well with M&E services. There was a lot of contractor design, specification was often by performance rather than by specified products, and detailed technical knowledge was required to describe and cost M&E installations.

Both DB&E and L&E realised this in the 1960s and worked to develop knowledge and capacity. Partners, Bill Fussell in DB&E and Alan Berryman in L&E, were made responsible for establishing and running M&E departments in their respective firms. Fussell was also responsible for compiling the first edition of *Spon's Mechanical & Electrical Services Price Book* in 1968 and *The Measurement of Engineering Services,* published in 1971. L&E developed a speciality in power station, industrial engineering, petrochemical and other projects with a high proportion of M&E installations.

Since the work required skills in measurement and technical design, the staff was often drawn from both quantity surveying and engineering backgrounds and the engineers were drawn from design and contracting. Because the work was so different from building quantity surveying, the M&E staff tended to work as a separate team and were, generally, not fully integrated with building teams, although they would be often, but not always, working on the same projects.

In 1970, Derek Mott and Peter Green, mechanical engineers, both with DB&E and Don Wall, an electrical engineer, decided to set up as a specialist firm of Mechanical and Electrical Quantity Surveyors in Victoria called Mott Green & Wall (MGW). They shared space with quantity surveyors VJ

Mendoza & Partners and did a lot of work with them, mainly on private commercial work, including major commercial projects like London Bridge City, and the Broadgate development at Liverpool Street Station.

In the 1980s, MGW was sold to a venture capital company and the founding partners left over the next few years. In the early 1990s, their owners went bankrupt but MGW was trading profitably and the joint managing directors, Ken Chesshire and Barry Nugent, negotiated a buy-out with the receiver. Convinced of the value of 'the brand', they retained the MGW name.

With the recovery in the mid-1990s, the newly independent firm flourished, working with Stuart Lipton's firm, Stanhope, and other developers. By the end of the decade, MGW was 30 strong and often worked alongside DLE on prestige commercial developments. Eventually the idea of a merger was raised. And not for the first time; MGW had been approached before by other large firms of quantity surveyors but had always resisted, often because the MGW name would be subsumed. Rob Smith and Paul Morrell and Chesshire and Nugent were the main participants in the merger discussions and, in May 1999, MGW became part of Davis Landon as Davis Langdon Mott Green & Wall.

The merger brought together two of the major firms of quantity surveyors in London commercial property construction. It undoubtedly added to the workload of both firms, although some clients may have liked them to remain separate, critiquing each other's work. In staff terms, MGW had a team of 30 and DLE had around 15. Total staff numbers are now over 100 with two thirds in London and the remainder spread across the UK and now in the Middle East. Around 20 per cent of the current staff are engineers, 40 to 50 per cent come from contracting backgrounds; a minority are qualified quantity surveyors.

The Davis Langdon MGW service offering is similar in purpose to core quantity surveying but focused on M&E services and the particular ways of working in that sector of the industry. Where it differs is in the design support that they offer on projects. MGW surveyors provide a technical service to clients on M&E issues; they also undertake full design critiques and design reviews and audits. Around three quarters of MGW projects are joint appointments with Davis Langdon, the remainder are direct appointments, often with other firms of quantity surveyors.

Legal Support Services

The firm's interest in legal related services comes from its historic involvement in building procurement and contractual matters. Geoff Trickey was writing in

Barry Nugent, Engineering Services.

the technical press in the 1970s on contractual issues and in the early 1980s was an adviser on the then new Association of Consultant Architects (ACA) form of contract.[3] In 1983, Trickey produced the first edition of *The Presentation and Settlement of Contractors' Claims,* published by E&FN Spon, publishers of the firm's *Price Books.* A number of other partners were also involved in legal matters, principally as expert witnesses, on construction disputes and claims both in the UK and internationally. But this interest and involvement was seen as an adjunct to quantity surveying practice; it enhanced the firm's reputation but was not perceived as a separate service.

In the 1960s and 1970s, there was a belief, at least among many architects, that quantity surveyors were particularly well qualified to advise on quasi-legal construction matters. This probably resulted from a combination of the

Broadgate, Skidmore Owings & Merrill.
Photographer: Roman von Gotz/Bildarchiv
Monheim/arcaid.co.uk.

Mark Hackett, Legal Support Services.

increased complexity of some building projects, the disinclination of architects to get involved in these matters and the virtual non-involvement of the legal profession in the industry at that stage. There was also genuine interest by some quantity surveyors in the private sector like Trickey and Roger Knowles and an important advisory role by quantity surveyors in the public sector, in central government ministries and agencies and local authorities.

In the early 1990s, Mark Hackett, then an associate in Trickey's team decided to take a more focused approach to legal issues in construction and was encouraged to do so. While continuing to work in a senior quantity surveying role (his projects included the refurbishment of the Mansion House in the City of London and projects for Amersham International), Hackett enrolled on a, then fairly new, MSc course in Construction Law at King's College, London. He qualified in 1994, by which time he was a partner of DLE.

Hackett proceeded to develop the legal support services work. The intention was to establish it as a distinct service line rather than as a side interest for individuals but, unlike some quantity surveyors involved in construction claims and disputes, the intent was to work with, rather than compete with, lawyers and this is still the case. Legal support services became a distinct profit centre in 1994.

In the early days, it was difficult to recruit appropriately qualified staff to this newish discipline. Ian Robinson, now a partner, joined with both quantity surveying and legal qualifications from public service in 1995. A later recruit in 1998 was Geoffrey Ashworth, former head of dispute resolution and a long standing partner of MDA (Monk Dunstone Associates), and highly respected in both construction and legal circles. At the time he joined Davis Langdon, Ashworth was also President of the QS Division of the RICS.[4]

An increasing incidence of legal disputes and the increasing demand for robust legal advice emerged in the late 1970s and early 1980s. Prior to that, claims and disputes occurred but were often resolved by negotiation or arbitration. And advice on procurement and contractual matters was, by and large, the province of quantity surveyors.

This started to change in the 1970s and by the 1980s a number of major law firms had partners, and eventually whole departments, dedicated to construction matters. It is interesting to note that *Building* magazine and *The Architects' Journal* had virtually no coverage of legal issues in the 1970s which is certainly not the case today. The Society of Construction Law was established in 1983 and has members from the legal profession and the construction industry, including a number of Davis Langdon partners and staff.

Legal support often attracts higher daily fee rates than many of the firm's other services, association with the legal world being generally more lucrative than being part of the construction industry. There is a nice story of Hackett being dissuaded from charging a particular daily rate that was on offer because it was higher than the senior partner of Davis Langdon would have charged at the time.

Like a number of 'new' services, legal support is not restricted to London but it is probably true to say that much of the expertise and resources and most of the big jobs are London based. Other offices where expert witness and similar services are part of the offering include Cardiff, Liverpool and Southampton. David Murphy in Southampton is on the RICS President's panel of adjudicators. Work overseas is an important component of the Legal support team's work. Recent major commissions include projects in the Far East, South America, Eastern Europe and, of course, the Middle East.

In 2001, Trickey and Hackett collaborated on a second edition of *The Presentation and Settlement of Contractors Claims* and a third edition is in preparation. In 2003, Hackett and others from the legal support team took on the editorship of the Aqua Group publications, publishing *Pre-contract Practice and Contract Administration* in 2003 and *Procurement, Tendering and Contract Administration,* in 2006.[5] Members of the team are represented on industry bodies and contribute to the technical press. In 2008 the group has six partners, 25 staff and a turnover of £4 million. Mark Hackett retired from Davis Langdon in 2009.

Management Consulting

Like Legal Support Services, Davis Langdon Management Consulting (DLMC) is 'home grown' and has its origins in a consultancy group established as an adjunct to the DB&E Cost Research Department in the early 1980s. It was founded by the author and developed by Meikle and John Connaughton, who joined in 1985.

Meikle joined the firm in 1979 and, apart from general work on cost research activities, he was charged with developing a Civil Engineering price book as a companion to the firm's other price books.[6] He was also encouraged to pursue and take on appointments for work that was construction and cost related but not mainstream quantity surveying. This sometimes sat uncomfortably with a tradition of providing advice more or less free of charge in order to attract quantity surveying work. Generally, however, consultancy work was non-project and usually for clients, or departments of clients, who did not use quantity surveyors.

In its first six months, two projects came along that were significant in what was to become the Consultancy Group's development. The first was an appointment to provide cost advice to Energy Conscious Design (now ECD Architects) on a study of passive solar house design; the second was to act as UK experts for an annual international cost comparison exercise run by the European Statistical Office (Eurostat), based in Luxembourg.

The client for the passive solar work was the Energy Technology Support Unit (ETSU) of the Department of Energy and the study led to a series of research and demonstration projects on low energy building design through the 1980s and 1990s with the Consultancy Group providing a range of cost, economic, market and, latterly, technical consultancy. The theme continues with DLMC's work with the Carbon Trust, the Waste and Resources Action Plan (WRAP) and their championing of sustainability in the firm. Eurostat is still a client of the firm 30 years later although the firm now coordinates the whole exercise, now involving over 30 countries, as well as providing the UK input.

By 1985 the group had their own identity and a distinct letterhead and in 1988, with the merger with L&E, Meikle became a partner and the group became a 'branch' office, with around ten people, based in London.

At the end of the 1980s, there was much talk about the implications of the Single European Market, to be launched on 1 January 1992.[7] The Construction Industry Research and Information Association (CIRIA) appointed the Group to research and write guides for UK construction professionals to the construction industries of France and Italy. This was followed by the RIBA commissioning guides to architectural practice in the same two countries.[8] The Group was also commissioned by the firm to look at opportunities for DLE in Europe. In the early 1990s, the Association of Consulting Engineers (ACE) commissioned consultancy to produce guides to the market for engineering consultancy services in the UK, Ireland, Spain and Portugal.

In retrospect, the industry's view of opportunities for UK firms in Europe was rather too optimistic. National markets were well protected and there were, and are still, significant barriers to entry: language, culture, professional practice and the like. The commissions, however, provided excellent grounding in market studies in the construction industry and useful market intelligence for the firm. It also provided sound credentials for a study of the QS profession commissioned by the RICS, *QS 2000, The Future Role of the Quantity Surveyor*.

In 1993 the Group was appointed by CIRIA to prepare an industry guide to value management. This was followed by *Value by Competition*, a guide to the

Jim Meikle, Management Consulting.

competitive selection of construction consultants and a number of other industry good practice and guidance documents. Following the publication of the Latham Report in 1994, a series of task groups were set up to compile or oversee the preparation of industry guides and codes of practice. The Consultancy Group was appointed to support production of three of these.

In the 1990s, as part of their market-orientated approach, the UK government increasingly withdrew from active involvement in construction research and research management. The research traditionally managed or undertaken by the Building Research Establishment, an agency of DoE, was progressively opened to other organisations and, eventually, BRE was privatised; and in 1998, the government increasingly turned to the private sector to manage and undertake the government's construction research programme.

Davis Langdon Consultancy, the new name for the Group became a major contributor to the research programme, initially undertaking research projects, then developing research strategies and, eventually, managing the greater part of the total programme. In the early 2000s, income from managing construction research represented more than half of DLC's income and regularly featured in Davis Langdon's top ten clients by value. But the end was coming for significant government support for construction research and the programme ended in 2006.

In 2004, the firm was appointed to act as National Change Agent on the Office of the Deputy Prime Minister's (ODPM's) social housing improvement programme.[9] In 2006, John Connaughton was charged by the Management Board with championing sustainability in the firm. Rob Smith and others were keen that the whole firm was informed and capable of advising on all aspects of sustainability. This built on Consultancy's work over two decades on related topics including, low energy buildings, renewable and alternative energy technologies, waste management, embodied energy and CO_2 and environmental research policy and management.

Meikle retired in 2005 and Connaughton, who had taken over as managing partner of what had become Davis Langdon Management Consulting (DLMC) in 2004 continued. Andy Garbutt joined as a partner in 2005 and, in 2007, a group led by Russell Poynter-Brown joined from Dearle & Henderson. DLMC now has a total complement of 26 people in three offices around the country. Its turnover in 2008 was £3.8 million.

Report on Architectural Practice in Italy, for the RIBA, 1991. Courtesy RIBA Publishing, www.ribapublishing.com.

Specification and Design Management

Nick Schumann and Dave Smith met at primary school in the 1960s and have been friends and colleagues ever since. They both became quantity surveyors, working with contractors, and they both went to work overseas in the 1970s. Schumann worked in the Middle East and Hong Kong and, in the 1980s, worked on the Hong Kong & Shanghai Bank headquarters building in Hong Kong, designed by Foster & Partners. Smith worked in the Middle East, mainly in Saudi Arabia. In 1986, back in the UK, they decided to set up on their own as Schumann Smith, Quantity Surveyors.

Initially their main work was for contractors preparing interim valuations, final accounts and claims but, shortly after setting up, they were approached by Foster & Partners to work with them on the new Stansted airport. The Hong Kong Bank project had not been straightforward and Fosters were sure that closer engagement with the contracting industry in the preparation of their documentation was important. Schumann Smith were seen as people who could help bridge that gap between design and construction. They worked on Stansted for three and a half years. Simultaneously they were working as quantity surveyors and had grown to 12 people, with the split of staff and workload roughly three quarters, quantity surveying, and one quarter, specifications. The business was doing well but in 1990 the recession struck.

Work disappeared more or less overnight, the staff were found other jobs and paid off and, by 1992, Schumann Smith was back to its founders. Schumann and Smith struggled on, surviving on small and infrequent commissions and their savings. In 1993, the phone rang: it was Foster & Partners, again. They were working on the new Chek Lap Kok airport in Hong Kong and asked if Schumann Smith could help with the specifications. They worked on the project for the next two years.

When the recession was over and the industry was starting to recover, the two partners decided that they would concentrate on specification consulting. Preparing specifications was something that many quantity surveyors did, including DB&E and L&E, as part of their role in compiling project documentation but it was not something that they claimed an expertise in. Schumann Smith was to change that.

Two projects for Foster & Partners, Stansted and Chek Lap Kok, had successively established and rescued Schumann Smith and they were to continue to work for Fosters and firms that were founded by ex-Fosters' people. By the late 1990s they had grown to 14 strong, all specification

Top: Nick Schumann.
Bottom: Dave Smith.

writers, and moved to larger premises in Stevenage. They were beginning to think about further expansion and the need for partners or investors.

Nick Schumann knew Paul Morrell through working with Fosters and felt that the firms might be 'a good fit'. In 1999 they spoke at a *Building* magazine reception and agreed to meet for lunch. Morrell and DLE were then involved in merger talks with Poole Stokes & Wood, Mott Green & Wall and NBW Crosher & James. Despite that, discussions were opened and went well and Schumann and Smith became partners of DLE on May 1 2000.

Since 2000, Schumann Smith, which retained the name post-merger, operating as Davis Langdon Schumann Smith, has grown and diversified. They now have over 40 people across the UK and operate in the Middle East and in South Africa and Australia, in joint venture with the DLSI local practices. They have developed a sophisticated software, the Integrated Construction Suite, that collects and collates all project information. They provide design management services to their architect clients. And turnover has grown from £900,000 before the merger to over £6 million in 2008. Davis Langdon Schumann Smith are currently working on The Grand Museum of Egypt, designed by Heneghan Peng Architects, the Specification Manual for the London 2012 Olympics and a project by Snøhetta at Ground Zero in New York.

Value, Planning and Risk

Michael Dallas was recruited in late 1997 to champion value in the firm; he had been with Hanscombs for ten years providing a value management service. Davis Langdon wanted Dallas to introduce value based thinking throughout the firm. For his first year, he travelled round the firm training quantity surveyors to run workshops. This was very effective in instilling the thinking but, when workshops or reports were required, more often than not it was Dallas who was asked to provide them; it was difficult to get the surveyors out of their primary role as cost managers. Value management was not entirely new to Davis Langdon. Tim Carter, from the Chester office and a project management enthusiast, had run workshops for a number of clients and projects for some years. But he was committed to project management and encouraged Dallas to join the firm. They knew each other from the Association of Project Managers (APM) and had represented the APM on an international promotional tour a couple of years earlier.

The Value team grew steadily over the next few years and continued to provide both internal training and external consultancy services. They were some six strong when Harpy Lally, the current group head, joined

Opposite top left: The Millennium Dome,
Greenwich, Richard Rogers & Partners.
Opposite top right: St Mary Axe,
Foster & Partners.
Photographer: Nigel Young.
Opposite bottom: Alexandria Library, Snøhetta.
Above: Michael Dallas, Value, Planning and Risk.

in 2001. The range of services was also gradually extended, initially to Risk Management and, in 2004, taking on the championing of DLivering Success. This is a project monitoring and evaluation process that had emerged from the Scottish Parliament project and the subsequent inquiry. The partners, and particularly Paul Morrell, were convinced that firms like Davis Langdon could not be passive observers of project failures and needed to have processes and procedures that would warn when projects were slipping into difficulty.

In 2006, the Value and Risk team was joined by a small planning and programming group that had been part of the project management team. In 2008, the Value Planning and Risk team has some 30 people, including the Planning team. They have an annual turnover of some £3.5 million, mostly with Davis Langdon clients.

Commentary

The diversification of quantity surveyors into other services was identified in *QS 2000*, written by the Davis Langdon & Everest Consultancy Group, now Davis Langdon Management Consulting, in 1991.[10] The report noted that

> Services will embrace the entire operating cycle of built assets from inception
> through design, construction, occupation and maintenance to disposal.
> Major service areas will be value management, procurement management
> and financial management, linked and organised by information technology.
> Specialist services will be provided, under a surveying umbrella, and these will
> include such areas as taxation, law, insurance, and market forecasting.

Much of this had happened: there were specialist firms like James R Knowles, in claims and dispute resolution, Mott Green & Wall, in mechanical and electrical services engineering, and Crosher & James, in taxation, and major firms like Gardiner & Theobald were established providers of project management services.

Arguably, Davis Langdon was relatively slow off the mark but over the past 20 years has developed, or acquired, an impressive range of non-core services. One thing that has not happened is that the services are provided "under a surveying umbrella". The term quantity surveyor is rarely used in the description or title of Davis Langdon or the other major firms, most preferring the term "cost management" or describing themselves as "construction consultants".

What is called "core" or "specialist" has also varied over time and will probably change again in the future. Cost Management and Project

Management are currently perceived as parallel core services. But Project Management only emerged as a distinct service line in the late 1980s and has been developed and presented at different times as both a separate Project Management, and as an integrated Cost and Project Management, service. It is also slightly odd to include engineering services as a specialist service since it is primarily a type of cost management but it is cost management undertaken by specialists. Bringing the specialist services together in Davis Langdon will no doubt reveal synergies in methods and tools and lead to interesting internal collaborations, if not 'mergers'.

Davis Langdon's offerings in Management Consulting, Legal Support and Value, Planning and Risk are essentially 'home grown' or, at least, developed in-house; Banking, Tax and Finance, Engineering Services and Specification and Design Management are largely acquisitions as a result of mergers in the late 1990s; and Building Surveying and CDM Consultancy have emerged in recent years from a realisation that the firm had acquired specialist resources, partly from mergers and partly from local needs.

Interestingly, the large, mainly accountancy-based, management consultants ventured into construction related services in the 1980s but by 2000 had more or less withdrawn from the sector, probably because there was too much competition from lower cost base construction industry consultants, like Davis Langdon. The large consultants are still involved in tax and financial services related to construction but less so in other fields. They are still, however, the consultants of choice for high level, strategic corporate or project consultancy and that is a challenge for the construction based consultants.

One of the management issues for a multi-disciplinary firm is cross-selling: the ability of one service to sell another service to their clients. The opportunity of this was a major attraction in a number of the specialist services mergers, for example, the Davis Langdon merger with NBW Crosher & James. There was a belief that cross selling would happen automatically but, by and large, it has not.

Sometimes one service was reluctant to promote another because they got work from a competitor and were more enthusiastic about that relationship than fostering the in-house service. Why would you promote Davis Langdon tax consultants when you get quantity surveying work from large firms of accountants who also do construction tax consultancy, or Davis Langdon building surveying when you get work from property consultants with their own building surveying departments? At other times, individuals or groups were uncomfortable or unsure about Davis Langdon offering a particular service and reluctant to promote it. The focus nowadays is on providing integrated solutions rather than selling.

It is a necessary characteristic of quantity surveyors that they be adaptable. Most, but not all, of the specialist services adopted in Davis Langdon have been developed by quantity surveyors but subsequent staff has not necessarily been from the same background. There is a tendency for specialists to become ever more specialist and the skills and knowledge of the founders are replaced by a new set of more focused, more directly relevant 'experts'. The advantages of this are evident but it may be at the expense of some of the adaptability that created the specialism. Initially the great thing was that, at least, the specialist could understand what the core service was even if the core service only had a hazy understanding of the specialism.

It is virtually certain that the range and contribution of specialist services will increase; Program Management and Construction ICT are currently being developed. But it is probable also that the 'rule' of not venturing into Design or Construction will be maintained. New services may emerge from the interests of individuals in the firm or strategic decisions but the need to obtain critical mass quickly argues for mergers or acquisitions rather than organic growth.

Specialist services have only recently been brought together into a single group and representatives of particular services are discovering that they have knowledge and skills in common with other services. In addition, the "One Firm One Future" initiative has removed many of the barriers to internal collaboration.

1   Capital allowances were introduced at the end of the nineteenth century to encourage industrial investment; they were originally known as "mills and factories allowance". Industrial buildings allowances replaced the mills and factory allowance in 1946. A new simplified system of capital allowances was introduced in 1971 and this became the basis of the Crosher & James' business model.
2   There are smaller groups or individuals in Edinburgh, Leeds, London, Manchester and Peterborough.
3   Trickey was a partner, 1967 to 1993, and joint senior partner, 1988 to 1993.
4   Ashworth died suddenly in 2003.
5   The Aqua Group series was first published in 1960 and has been republished under different titles over the years. It is intended for young construction professionals but is a useful guide for practitioners of all ages.
6   *The Civil Engineering Price Book* was eventually published, five years later, and is now a member of the UK annual price book series.
7   The Single European Act that led to the single market was signed by Margaret Thatcher in 1986.

8   At the same time, Reading University produced companion guides to Germany and WS Atkins produced guides to Portugal and Spain.

9   ODPM is now the Department for Communities and Local Government (DCLG).

10   *QS2000, The Future Role of the Quantity Surveyor*, was published by the Quantity Surveyors Division of the RICS in June 1991.

Chapter Nine

A Knowledge-based Firm

It is common nowadays for firms of quantity surveyors to publish in the technical press and to comment on industry practices and procedures. But it was not always like that and Davis Langdon, and, particularly, the Davis bit of the firm, was in the forefront of presenting a public face for quantity surveying and construction economics from the 1930s. Nowadays, publication is often seen as an aspect of marketing; then it was perceived as research, although its profile-raising potential was always recognised by, at least, some in the practice.

In 1938, Owen Davis was asked to produce a feature on building prices for *The Architects' Journal (AJ)* and this was to be the start of the firm's long standing relationship. It is reproduced opposite.

At the same time, Davis was lecturing at the Architectural Association and Cambridge University and had strong links with many of the emerging young architects of the day. In the early 1940s, Davis & Belfield took on the job of running *The Architects' Journal* Information Centre, which undertook to answer architects' questions on any aspect of the building industry. Owen Davis notes that the "technique was to phone up the experts and put the question to them and the opening gambit was 'I am speaking on behalf of the Director of *The Architects' Journal* Information service; one of our readers wishes to know…?'" He went on to comment "I have often wondered how the staff offices and ministerial experts who dashed off so obligingly to find out the answers for this high powered organisation, would have reacted if they had known that the lordly person 'speaking on behalf of the Director' was none other than Charles Wheeler, office boy, whose recent insistence on £1 per week had nearly lost him a job."[1]

In 1947, DB&E took over the editorship of *E&FN Spon's Architects' and Builders' Price Book* for its 74th edition, published in January 1948, apparently in response to a critical review by Owen Davis of the previous edition.[2] The book was "entirely revised to reflect the conditions prevailing in the building industry after the 1939–1945 war". The table reproduced overleaf sets out the 'Cubes', estimated prices per cubic foot, included in the first edition edited by DB&E.

The prices are expressed in pre-decimal currency and Imperial units of measurement, hence 3s 4d per cubic foot for 'Assembly Rooms' is equivalent to just less than £6 per cubic metre or £24 per square metre (assuming a storey height of four metres). A more recognisable building type at the same rate (3s 4d per cubic foot) is 'Schools', which *Spon's* 2008 indicates at between £850 and £1,500 per square metre.[3] The notes to the table point out the shortcomings of using prices per cubic unit of measurement but it was very much industry practice of the day and was not replaced by prices per square unit until the 1960s.[4] As an aside, it was only after the Second World War that quantity

Opposite: Owen Davis' feature in the *AJ*, 27 January 1938.

The following Supplement is the product of many months of work on the part of this JOURNAL and its collaborators, Messrs. Davis and Belfield, PP.,I.S.I., Chartered Quantity Surveyors, who have been asked to undertake the difficult task of creating a new PRICES section. It represents, within obvious limitations and so far as the advice of a number of experts can make it, the most precise and detailed statement of current prices obtainable. We are particularly asked by its compilers to invite readers who use it to forward their reactions (criticism, we hope) to the Editor at 9 Queen Anne's Gate, London, S.W.1, so that adjustments may be made where necessary. The whole of the information is copyright.

PRICES

PART 1

CURRENT MARKET PRICES OF MATERIALS
BY DAVIS AND BELFIELD, P.A.S.I.

CONCRETOR

Cements

All delivered in paper bags (20 to the ton) free and non-returnable.

		4 Tons and over	Min. 80 ton freights F.A.S. Safe wharf in River Thames, London area
Portland	..	per ton 42/–	38/–
Rapid hardening	..	„ 48/–	44/–
Water repellent	..	„ 72/–	68/–

			1 ton upwards
Colorcrete rapid hardening, Nos. 1 and 2		per ton	66/–
Snowcrete	..	„	175/–

		1–10 cwts.	11–15 cwts.	16–20 cwts.	1 ton and upwards
Ciment Fondu, delivered Central London area	per cwt.	7/9	7/3	6/–	6/–

Aggregate and Sands (Full Loads)

¾" Unscreened ballast	..	..	per yard cube	6/3
¼" (Down) Washed, crushed and graded shingle			„ „	6/9
¾" (Down) Ditto	..	..	„ „	7/9
¾" Broken brick	..	..	„ „	10/6
¾" Ditto	..	..	„ „	11/0
Washed pan breeze	..	..	„ „	5/3
Coke breeze 1" to dust	..	..	„ „	13/6
¾" Sharp washed sand	..	..	„ „	8/6
White Silver Sand for white cement (one ton lots) per ton 25/–				

(For Sands for Bricklaying and Plastering see respective trades)

Pavings

Brick hardcore	..	..	..	per yard cube	2/9
Clean furnace clinker and boiler ashes	..	„ „			3/6
Coarse gravel for paths	..	..	„ „		6/9
Fine ditto	..	..	..	„ „	9/6
Clean granite chippings	..	..	per ton		18/6
Red quarry tiles, 6" × 6" × ¾"		per yard super			6/–
Buff ditto, 6" × 6" × ¾"	..	..	„ „		6/6
Hard red paving bricks	..	..	..	per 1,000	150/–

Reinforcement

Basis price for mild steel rods, ¾" diameter and upwards, from London stocks .. .. .. per ton £17 10 0

Extras for :—

⅜" and ½" diameter	..	..	..	„	10/–
⅜"	„	..	..	„	15/–
¼"	„	..	..	„	20/–
⅛"	„	..	..	„	30/–
⅛"	„	..	..	„	40/–
⅛"	„	..	..	„	60/–
Lengths of 40 ft. to 45 ft.	..	..	„		10/–
„ 45 ft. to 50 ft.	..	..	„		15/–

CONCRETOR—(continued)

Sundries

Retarding liquid, in 5-gallon drums (for exposing aggregate) per gallon	20/–	Ex Warehouse, Southwark Bridge.
Ditto, (for obtaining a bond) per gallon	22/6	Drums chargeable and credited, if returned.

BRICKLAYER

Common Bricks

Rough stocks ..	..	..	..	per 1,000	73/–
Third stocks	..	..	..	„	54/6
Mild stocks	..	..	..	„	71/6
Sand limes	..	..	..	„	50/–
* Phorpres pressed Flettons..		..		„	46/3
* „ keyed Flettons ..		..		„	48/3
† Bespres Flettons		..		„	49/–
Blue Staffordshire wirecuts ..		..		„	165/–
Lingfield engineering wirecuts		..		„	95/–
Breeze fixing bricks	..	..		„	57/6
Firebricks, best Stourbridge 2½"		..		„	155/–
„ „ 3"		..		„	190/–

* At King's Cross. For delivery in W.C. district add 4/3 per 1,000.
† Delivered in London area.

Facing and Engineering Bricks

Sand Limes, No. 1	..	..	..	per 1,000	85/–
„ No. 2	..	..	..	„	70/–
*Phorpres rustic Flettons	..	..		„	66/3
Marston bark rustic	..	..		„	64/–
Midhurst Whites	..	..	..	„	82/6
Hard stocks, firsts	..	..		„	95/–
„ seconds..	..	..		„	88/–
Sand-faced, hand-made reds	..	..		„ from	115/–
„ machine-made reds	..	..		„ from	110/–
Red rubbers (9½-in.) ..	..	..		„	300/–
Hunziker	..	..	..		„	67/6
„ (coloured) ..	..	..		„ from	82/6
Dunbricks (concrete), multi reds, ex works				„	72/–
„ „ multi lavender, ex works		..		„	75/–
Southwater engineering No. 1 (first quality red pressed)		..		„	145/–
Southwater engineering No. 2 (second quality red pressed)		..		„	125/–
Blue pressed	..	..	..	„	171/–

* At King's Cross. For delivery in W.C. district add 4/3 per 1,000.
Discount if accompanied by order for pressed 2/– per 1,000.

CUBES

	Per ft. cube		Per ft. cube
	s. d.		s. d.
Assembly Rooms	3 4	Flats	3 10
Asylums	3 9	Garages	1 11
Banks	4 1	Hospitals	4 0
Barns	1 4½	Hotels	5 2
Barracks.	3 0	Houses	2 9½
Baths (Public)	3 9	Laboratories	3 9
Chapels (Plain)	2 10½	Laundries	3 9
Churches	3 11	Libraries	4 4
Cinemas	4 3	Municipal Buildings . .	4 7½
Colleges	4 7	Offices	4 0
Cow-houses	2 1½	Police Stations	3 9
Crematoriums	5 9	Post Offices	3 8
Dairies	3 3	Public Houses	3 10
Drill Halls	2 2½	Schools	3 4
Factories — Mills, etc.:		Sheds.	1 5½
Light, Single Storey	1 11	Shops	3 9
Heavy, Several Stories	2 10½	Theatres	5 2
Fire Brigade Stations . .	3 9		

surveyors felt that they should, or could, suggest what buildings might cost before they were built, rather than tell people what they had cost afterwards.

All of this interest in writing and teaching and the associated research was to become a cornerstone of the firm's services and its public image. There have always been a few people in the firm who felt that, by publishing prices, etc., the firm was giving away its knowledge base, 'its crown jewels' but the 'put it in the public domain' policy prevailed and still prevails.

Cost Analysis and Cost Planning

In the 1950s, the government, initially on the post-war schools programme, introduced the idea of cost analysis and cost planning. The stimulus was Stirrat Johnson-Marshall, Chief Architect at the Ministry of Education, asking a young quantity surveyor, James Nisbet, why the costs of schools varied so much.[5] Nisbet had been with Johnson-Marshall at Hertfordshire County Council in the late 1940s and they had started to investigate why apparently 'standard' buildings varied so much in cost. "They could establish that the same size of primary school cost, say £100 in North Yorkshire and £300 in Middlesex, they had that range of costs. What they couldn't get was any rational reason why." [6]

Approximate estimating rates per cubic foot from *Spon's Architects' and Builders' Price Book*, 1948.

The idea that you could analyse cost information from tendered or completed projects to get information on which to base estimates for future projects may seem obvious now but it was not then; indeed the ideas were resisted by many quantity surveyors and, for some time, by the RICS. Some at least of the early partners in both L&E and DB&E were, however, notable exceptions. Tom Every worked in the Ministry of Works during the war and was heavily involved in planning for the post-war era; Owen Davis was fascinated by all innovation in quantity surveying processes and practice; John Parrinder, an early post-war partner of DB&E was heavily involved in the development of the Building Research Station and the Cost Research Panel of the RICS that led to the setting up of the Building Cost Information Service (BCIS); Colin Brearley established a cost planning department in L&E in the 1960s. A number of partners subsequently sat on the board of the BCIS and their attitudes and ideas influenced others in both firms.

Government was the main driver of cost planning via the various systems of cost limits. These appeared first for schools but were then developed for public housing (eventually emerging as the Housing Cost Yardstick), hospitals and university buildings (Tom Every was a member of a University Grants Committee in 1954). Knowledge of, and skills in manipulating, the various cost limit regimes were essential attributes of quantity surveyors working on public projects and both DB&E and L&E had enviable reputations on housing, health and educational buildings. And, again, articles were published on the operation of the various cost limit systems; Geoff Trickey wrote articles on the Housing Cost Yardstick in the *AJ*.[7]

The Cost and Information Library and Department

A Cost Information and Research Group was set up in the early 1960s by Dick Milborne, then an Associate of DB&E, with a particular interest in cost planning.[8] One of his team, Don Lake was the first full-time member of staff of the new group. Later in the 1960s, Roger Howard took over the post, and he was followed in 1970 by David Wood. Wood was responsible for the production of internal design and cost studies and these became the forerunners of a series of articles produced for the *AJ*. He left the firm, briefly, in the mid-1970s when Brian Tysoe took over, assisted by Rob Smith, a young assistant surveyor recruited by Geoff Trickey. Wood returned in 1976 and variously worked on cost research and computer development. Other individuals who have headed or spent time in the department include Rob Smith (late 1970s, early 1980s), Jim Meikle (late 1970s, early 1980s), Simon Johnson (mid-1980s) and Neill Morrison (mid-1980s).

Core duties undertaken by the department include the preparation of cost and price indices and forecasts, cost analyses and reports and material for publication in the technical press. It also undertakes commissioned research where this is relevant to the firm's business.

The first qualified librarian, Mary Novak, was appointed in 1970. Originally the library was set up to centralise surveyors' own catalogue libraries but moved on to collect and collate an increasing number of reports, articles, statistics and cost analyses produced by various government departments and agencies, the BCIS and the technical press. 'Newer' partners, such as Geoff Trickey, were taking over the reins from Owen Davis in writing articles on a range of topics for the *AJ* and other magazines; they were also giving regular lectures to, mainly architectural, students and at industry events. All of this called for a well-organised library and an increase in the analysis, recording, storing and indexing of the firm's projects.

Novak left late in 1971 and Linda Williams joined in 1972 and stayed until 2004, becoming the first female associate in the firm in the 1980s. Rosemary Blackwell, the current librarian, continues the tradition of answering the most obscure questions by partners, staff, and outside enquirers. Library computerisation was started in the 1990s and most enquiries are now dealt with electronically but the paper files stand as a testament to an early and continuous commitment to the value of technical data and information and as an invaluable resource. The library has more than 3,000 cost analysis files on projects, by building type, going back to the 1950s and there is a unique collection of industry reports, data, standards and other documents. It is one of the best construction libraries in the country.

In January 1968, a weekly internal *Information Sheet* was published for the first time with the week's industry news summarised on one side of A4. 40 years on it is still produced each Friday, now, however, usually, on two sides. Initially, the newsheet was for internal circulation but it very quickly went out to selected colleagues and clients and became a 'must read'. When the first Davis Langdon Customer Satisfaction survey was undertaken in the 1990s, the newsheet was consistently recorded as one of the most distinctive, admired and appreciated of the firm's products. In 2008, weekly circulation is over 3,000, 1,500 electronically and the remainder in hard copy, although the latter is being discontinued. Since 2006, a bi-weekly *Knowledge Bulletin*, an internal technical briefing, has been produced.

Davis Belfield & Everest produced a number of *DB&E News* in the 1960s and a single edition in 1986. They contained reminiscences, technical information, details of the firm's projects and reports of social events and have been useful in compiling this history but their production was, to say the least, irregular. In March 1991, the first edition of *Grapevine*, an in-house staff journal, was produced. Issues initially ran to eight sides of A4 and appeared nine times a year but by the late 1990s they had increased in size to 16 or more pages but reduced in frequency to six editions per year and they declined in both size and frequency in subsequent years. *Grapevine* last appeared in 2006, largely superseded by the firm's intranet, summit, and the *Knowledge Bulletin*.

The purpose of *DB&E News* and *Grapevine* was to keep staff informed about the firm's jobs, professional developments, social events, etc.. In the 1990s there came increasing pressures to involve, as well as inform, staff in initiatives like Quality Assurance (achieved in London in 1992 and introduced in regional offices through the 1990s); Professional Development Reviews (introduced for graduates in 1991 and for all staff and partners by the late 1990s); Business Planning (introduced in 1997, partly as a prerequisite of IIP); and Investors in People, IIP (achieved in London in 1998).

Since 2004 the department has been developing a National Cost Database (NCDB). This comprises cost information in a variety of forms and from a variety of sources, all aggregated to cost planning items and in one location. It is delivered to surveyors as bi-annual consolidated schedules and is an essential source and cross-check for estimates and cost plans.

Davis Langdon now produces a weekly economic briefing written by a resident economist.

Cost and Price Indices and Forecasting

In the 1960s, quantity surveyors in the Ministry of Public Building and Works (MPBW), developed a method of calculating price level indices for building work from a sample of items in priced bills of quantities assessed against a standard pricing schedule. The method was adopted by the Building Cost Information Service (BCIS) of the RICS; it was also adopted by the newly formed DB&E Cost research department and from the late 1960s they compiled a tender price index, primarily from their own projects. The DB&E 'standard pricing schedule' was, of course, *Spon's Architects' and Builders' Price Book*. The MPBW, and now ONS (Office for National Statistics), the BCIS and the firm's indices have run in parallel ever since. They show broadly similar but not identical trends, reflecting the sample of projects included.

In November 1975, the firm produced the first of a new series of articles in the *AJ* entitled "Looking into the Future". They were to forecast

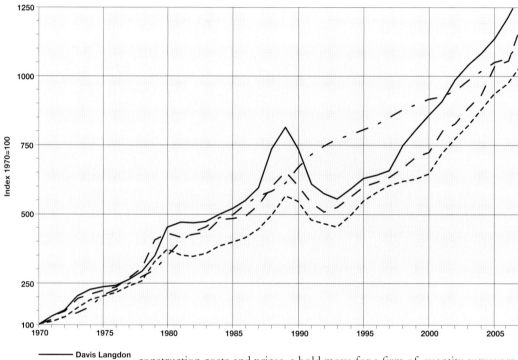

Davis Langdon ——
RPI — -
ONS — —
BCIS - - - -

construction costs and prices, a bold move for a firm of quantity surveyors, and in an architectural journal. In the introductory article, Geoff Trickey explained that they had been running tests for some time and noted "that many of the predictions have been wrong and it is only honest to suggest that this will continue; indeed, it may be said that this prediction is the only one that we can guarantee". It was brave at the time to suggest that construction costs could be predicted and for a number of years the DB&E forecast was the only one. More than 30 years later, the series, now running in *Building* magazine, is one of a number of forecasting features published by a range of firms and organisations but it is still as rigorous and respected as ever.

Forecasts were published quarterly and in a longer article than usual in February 1981, some of the background work on the indicators that informed their forecasts, in addition to drawing on the views of senior staff around the country, was discussed. Four indicators were presented: Contractors' new orders, Construction liquidations, Classified advertising in the *AJ* and something called the "DB&E market factor". The first two were, of course, based on official statistics and the third was based on data provided by the *AJ*. The last was of the firm's own devising and was calculated by dividing (deflating) their tender price index by their cost index to obtain a so-called market factor. By selecting a base date for the exercise at

Graph showing the three tender price indices (1970 to 2007) and the RPI.

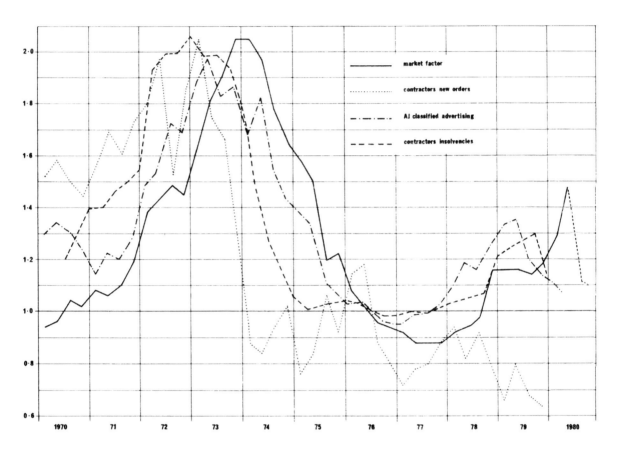

Legend:
- market factor
- contractors new orders
- AJ classified advertising
- contractors insolvencies

which the market was more or less in equilibrium, this meant that a factor of more than 1.0, and rising, suggested a buoyant market while a factor of less than 1.0, and falling, suggested a depressed market. The merit of all these indicators was that they indicated trends and allowed informed assumptions to be made. They were inevitably better at forecasting trends than turning points but provided, and still provide, a useful framework for the firm's cost estimating and cost planning. The articles published nowadays in *Building* magazine are described as Market Forecasts and provide an extensive commentary on national, regional and industry trends.

Articles in the Technical Press

Extract from the *AJ*, 25 February 1981, showing the four indicators for tender price forecasts.

In the late 1970s, DB&E produced an innovative series of articles in the *AJ* on the costs of different building types called Initial Cost Estimating (ICE). The series was researched and written by David Wood. The idea was to

DESIGN/COST SELECTION CHART   *worked example*   WAREHOUS

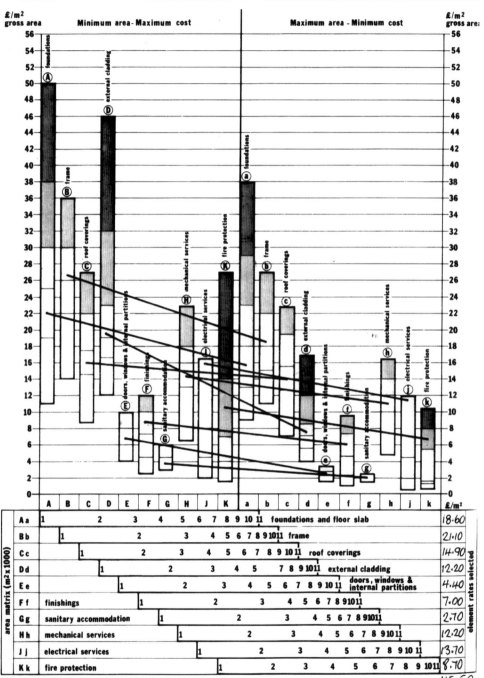

											£/m²
A a	1	2	3	4	5	6	7 8 9 10 11	foundations and floor slab			18·60
B b		1	2	3	4 5 6 7 8 9 10 11	frame					21·10
C c			1	2	3	4 5 6 7 8 9 10 11	roof coverings				14·90
D d				1	2	3 4 5	7 8 9 10 11	external cladding			12·20
E e					1	2	3	4 5 6 7 8 9 10 11	doors, windows & internal partitions		4·40
F f	finishings				1	2	3	4 5 6 7 8 9 10 11			7·00
G g	sanitary accommodation			1		2	3	4 5 6 7 8 9 10 11			2·70
H h	mechanical services				1	2	3	4 5 6 7 8 9 10 11			12·20
J j	electrical services			1		2	3	4 5 6 7 8 9 10 11			13·70
K k	fire protection				1	2	3	4 5 6 7 8 9 10 11			8·70

area matrix (m² x 1000)   *element rates selected*

Job name = *Sample warehouse*
Site location = *Macclesfield*
Gross floor area = 3500 m²
Final estimate = £ 383,000
(excluding external works)

rate/m² for selected warehouse = £ 115·50
extra for additional specification = £ 0·86
          116·36
adjusted by site location factor @ 0·89 = £103·56
update by × $\frac{\text{estimate date AJ tender index}}{\text{June 1977 AJ tender index}}$ $\frac{265}{251}$
∴ final estimated rate/m² for building = £ 109·33

improve the reliability of early stage cost estimates. A range of costs linked to indicative specifications and overall building size, was presented for the main building elements and guidance provided on how this information could be manipulated into a realistic project cost estimate. Wood was later responsible for translating the articles into computer based models that could be used in early stage discussions with clients and designers.

The diagram opposite illustrates a worked example of the ICE approach for warehouse building. The vertical scale is in £ per square metre gross floor area. The diagram is in two parts each comprising vertical bars showing plausible cost ranges for ten building elements; on the left, the bars relate to smaller warehouses in which rates per square metre will usually be higher; on the right, the bars relate to larger buildings. The subdivisions in the bars indicate different costs related to different specifications (brief notes on specification are provided in the article).

Given sketchy information, the type of building, gross floor area and broad ideas on specification, it was possible to come up with a realistic and soundly based cost estimate very quickly. More importantly, this was linked to specifications for the main elements and could be easily adjusted. The approach made the early estimating process more transparent and allowed designers and clients to see the effects of their decisions before serious design work was undertaken. ICE articles were produced for a range of building types, including offices, factories and housing, and the approach transferred readily to the computer.

The tradition of publishing cost estimating information continues with the Cost Model series in *Building* magazine. These are produced regularly and cover a wide range of building types and topical construction issues. In addition, the firm regularly contributes articles on methods of procurement and other aspects of industry practice. In 2008, some 40 plus articles were published, around 25 of these in *Building* magazine, the remainder in a range of other publications.

Spon's Price Books

Cyril 'Chippy' Smith was largely responsible for the production of *A&B Spon's* from shortly after 1947, when the book was taken over, until he retired in the 1980s. Initially, work on the book was undertaken by Owen Davis himself. With the book's success, Spon's encouraged the firm to expand the range of price books. The first of these was the *Mechanical & Electrical Services Price Book*.

It had become increasingly obvious to thinking quantity surveyors in the days of cost planning that they knew very little about, and were often not really involved

Extract from the *AJ*, 1 June 1977, showing the Initial Cost Estimating Element Design/Cost Selection Chart for Warehouses.

COST MODEL OFFICE REFURBISHMENT

A slowdown in the office market combined with an increasingly prominent sustainability agenda is creating opportunities for refurbishment specialists. **Simon Rawlinson** and **Max Wilkes** of Davis Langdon discuss how to maximise a building's value with a well-targeted refurbishment programme

01 / INTRODUCTION

Commercial development is concerned with optimising the capital value of property assets. Development is a high-risk business, involving a large investments, long project durations and a highly cyclical pattern of supply and demand. Total redevelopment is usually the preferred option in a rising market, as this makes the best use of a site and provides a product tailored to market expectations. However, for some projects, either timing or site constraints such as historic building status or the existing planning consent can mean that a refurbishment provides a better balance of risk and return.

Even in an office market as uncertain as the present one, tenants still need space. In responding to this, refurbishment projects have several advantages over new build. These include:

■ **Speed to market** Simplified planning, reduced demolition and the ability to reuse elements of the existing building can provide considerable programme advantages.

■ **Cash flow and tenant retention** Many city-centre schemes mix office, retail and sometimes residential uses, each with different lease terms. Refurbishment options often allow retail to be retained while upper floor space is reconfigured.

■ **Cost** Avoidance of total demolition and the reconstruction of major elements of the building fabric should result in capital cost savings of at least 20%, even on major projects.

■ **Retention of the value drivers of the original building** These may include permitted

development density and massing, parking allocations and, with older buildings, style and character. Refurbishment consents can also be obtained without an additional section 106 requirement for housing contributions and the like.

The interior of the Unilever House in central London, complete with this striking atrium. Opposite: The exterior. The architect was Kohn Pedersen Fox

■ **Sustainability** The reuse of the building fabric and improvements to the building's performance in use mean that the overall environmental impact of a refurbishment is likely to be lower than for a new-build.

High-profile refurbishment schemes in London, such as 125 Broad Street and 55 Baker Street, as well as projects in all major cities, show how reuse options continue to make financial sense.

In summary, the timing of lease expiries and the evolving needs of tenants mean that there will always be a demand for attractive, efficient space, even in a downturn. With the introduction of energy performance certificates from 2008 onwards, occupiers are expected to become even more aware of their energy consumption, prompting further investment in existing buildings to maintain their value.

Refurbishment options involve uncertainty but overall carry a smaller development risk, which can be mitigated further by varying the scope of the refurbishment investment in response to market demand. For developers, consultants and contractors with the skills, uncertain market conditions will create further opportunities to deliver value-adding solutions.

This cost model is concerned with large projects that involve the reconfiguration and extension of floorplates and services to provide the highest standard of accommodation. Many of the issues raised, however, also apply to smaller-scale refurbishments.

in, mechanical and electrical installations in buildings and that the costs of these were substantial and growing. In DB&E, Bill Fussell took a particular interest and in 1971 wrote a textbook on *The Measurement of Engineering Services*; Alan Berryman took a similar interest in L&E; and by the late 1960s, both firms had established specialist M&E departments. The first edition of *Spon's Mechanical and Electrical Services Price Book* was published in 1968.

Ten years later, a *Spon's Landscaping and External Works Price Book* was compiled, initially in association with Derek Lovejoy & Associates, Landscape Architects. And, in 1984, *Spon's Civil Engineering Price Book* was published to complete the set of the firm's UK price books. The last was looked on particularly askance by engineers (clients, consultants and contractors) who were all largely of the view that you could not estimate the cost of civil engineering work until after it was built, a view still common today.

The four UK price books have now been an established part of the UK construction scene for decades and for many the firm's name is synonymous with Spon's. Responsibility for detailed compilation of individual books is shared across the firm. The M&E and Civil Engineering books were originally written in London but subsequent production of the former was taken on by the Chester office and, more recently, Davis Langdon MGW; the latter was taken on by the Liverpool office. The Landscape book was originally written as a companion to Lovejoy's Design Guide; it is now sub-contracted to Sam Hassall's Landpro Landscape Surveyors.

It is difficult to get hold of accurate sales figures for competitors, but it seems that Spon's has been the market leader in UK construction price books for many years. The UK price books were computerised by David Wood in the 1980s and have been published with electronic (CD) versions for some time. Electronic publishing will inevitably develop and there is an increasing amount of construction cost information on the firm's intranet and website. Hard copy publishing has, however, proved remarkably resilient.

In DB&E's Chester office, in 1971, Andrew Thomson, the local partner, was interested in developing work internationally, particularly in Europe. He wrote a number of pieces for internal consumption and this was then built on by others to eventually become a European price section running to ten countries and around 100 pages and included in A&B Spon's until separate books were produced.

A *Spon's International Construction Costs Handbook* was published in 1988 and included 32 countries, 15 European. After the merger in 1988, the case was made for separate Asia Pacific and European books. The Asia Pacific region was now an important and distinct part of the firm. A first edition of the

Cover page of the Office Refurbishment Cost Model from *Building* magazine, 20 June 2008.

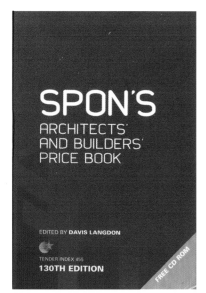

Asia Pacific book was published in 1994 and was a joint project between London and Singapore offices. Subsequent editions were produced by Singapore and published in 1997 and 2000, with a fourth edition planned for 2009. Europe was seen as a key target market and a first edition of *Spon's European Construction Costs Handbook* was published in 1992, a second edition in 1995 and a third in 2000.[9] The format of all the international books was broadly similar with the bulk taken by country sections and with each having an introductory essay and a final section with comparative data.

Other Publications

In 1983, E&FN Spon published *The Presentation and Settlement of Contractors' Claims* by Geoff Trickey. This was a result of Trickey's interest in legal aspects of construction and a forerunner of what was to become Davis Langdon Legal Support Services, established by Mark Hackett in the early 1990s. Hackett worked closely with Trickey in the 1980s, on quantity surveying and legal support projects, and was co-author on the second edition of the *Claims* book, published in 2001 (a third edition is in preparation).

Over the years, the firm has written or contributed to a number of important industry publications including *The UK Construction Challenge*, published by Lynton plc in 1993, and guidance documents for the National Audit Office. In addition, Davis Langdon Management Consulting has been responsible for over 50 published documents over the past 20 years, including industry best practice and guidance documents and market studies.

Computers and Computing

In 1963 the Development Group of Chartered Quantity Surveyors was formed "to investigate computer working to serve the profession and the Building Industry at large". The six founding firms were: Davis, Belfield & Everest, Dearle & Henderson, Franklin & Andrews, Gardiner & Theobald, EC Harris & Partners, and Langdon & Every. In 1966 six other firms were invited to join: Crosher & James, Gleeds, Reynolds & Young, JW Summers & Partners, and Widnell & Trollope. 40 odd years on, it is interesting to see that three of these firms, among the leading edge firms of the day, are now part of Davis Langdon LLP.

In 1980, the DB&E London office installed its first computers, a large Data General mini-computer (although not very 'mini' in today's terms) running the firm's accounts and a Commodore PET with 32k of memory and 5¼ inch

Spon's Architects' and Builders' Price Book.
© Spon Press.

floppy disks, each holding 343k of data. By the end of the 1980s, desktop machines were more widespread, originally Amstrads and later IBM PCs, there were, however, probably less than 20 in the London office and there was no network. Around the same time, the Initial Cost Estimating articles were put on computer, initially Texas Instruments hand-held programmable calculators and later written in Basic on the firm's first DEC mini-computer.

The Website and Intranet

The firm's first website, www.dle.co.uk, was created in 1996. It was only for the UK and was compiled in-house in HTML. In 1998, URLs were secured for the different regions internationally; these sites were also compiled in-house. The current website, www.davislangdon.com, was launched in March 2007; it was compiled using external designers and technical consultants but with in-house content management.

After a number of years gestation, an intranet was introduced in 2000, originally managed by the Professional Development team. The name 'Summit' was selected after a UK-wide competition and was, of course, related to the Everest part of the firm's name.[10] An updated version was launched in 2003, managed by the IT Department. This is the system that is still in place.

The firm now has a desktop learning system targeted at quantity surveyors and project managers that provides essential background on issues like sustainability. It presents issues and concepts that everyone in the firm should be aware of and provides a baseline set of information and requirements.

Research Commissions

Both DB&E and L&E undertook specialist research commissions and studies. L&E's work in the Middle East stems from a report prepared for British Petroleum in 1946 on their proposed programme of work in Iran. Professional Development also undertakes the regular *Contracts in Use* survey in association with the RICS and acts as the UK construction price expert for Eurostat, OECD and World Bank international comparison studies. They have undertaken consultancy commissions for a number of UK government departments and agencies and for commercial firms. The focus of the group, however, is primarily on supporting the knowledge base and the work of the firm and external research is a relatively small part of the group's work.

Spon's European Construction Costs Handbook.
© Spon Press.

Foresighting

In Summer 2000, Paul Morrell, senior partner, decided to charge a small group of six 'bright young things' with some 'blue skies thinking'. They were taken out of their teams for three months and asked to explore the strategic direction the firm should follow and propose solutions for how it might get there. The result was a variety of ideas and proposals on both technical and personnel issues; a number were adopted at least partly as a consequence of the group's work. The exercise was also successful in identifying future leaders, all six are now partners, albeit one with a competitor.

The idea was revived by Rob Smith in 2005 as the Foresight groups. A group is selected each year, drawn from all sides of the firm, geographically and client facing and support, and given a brief to think widely and deeply about the firm's future, professionally and as a business. They work through the year giving presentations to the Board and the senior partner attends their monthly meetings. The 2007 Foresight group looked at the sustainability agenda for the firm and came up with an award winning 'green cars' policy.

Professional Development in 2008

In 1998, Professional Development (PD) was formally recognised as one of five business support groups (the others are Finance, Business Development, Human Resources and IT) and the head of professional development was to be a partner. PD is currently led by Simon Rawlinson, a partner since 1999 and has almost 20 staff, 12 in London, four in Manchester and Birmingham and one in the Middle East.

Commentary

Davis Langdon is undoubtedly a knowledge based firm. For the past 60 years, the firm has been at the forefront of quantity surveying, construction economics and industry research and innovation. Since the 1960s, the firm has maintained both a technical library and a full time research group. Through in-house, practice based and commissioned research the firm has consistently been a contributor to industry knowledge and has mostly been happy to disseminate their knowledge widely.

The firm's publications, particularly in the *AJ* and, more recently, in *Building* magazine and *Spon's Price Books* are referred to throughout the industry and envied by their competitors. The commitment to internal communications from the newsheet in the 1960s to the intranet today has been consistent. The tradition of teaching and lecturing established by Horace Langdon in the 1920s and Owen Davis in the 1930s has continued over the years and partners and others regularly contribute to undergraduate and higher degree courses and to industry events.

The firm's work on cost planning, cost and price indices and forecasting, estimating and computer applications has always been at the front of quantity surveying practice. Rob Smith, the current senior partner, started his career in the cost research department and for more than 25 years as a partner has maintained an interest in, and support for, the department and its work. Professional development is a key element of Davis Langdon's Business Support.

1   Wheeler subsequently worked at Aldermaston and, in 1956, moved to Leeds to open one of the early post-war offices. He became a local partner in 1962 and retired in 1982.

2   E&FN Spon was established in London as a bookshop in 1834 by Baron de Spon, a French nobleman who had escaped the French Revolution. It began publishing books in 1862 and the first edition of *The Architects' and Builders' Price Book* was published in 1873. The firm is only the third editor in the book's 135 year history.

3   Available indices suggest that £24 per square metre is equivalent to £925 per square metre in 2008, at the low end of the Spon's range but comfortably within it.

4   The 1962/1963 edition of Spon's was the first to omit prices per cubic foot entirely.

5   Nisbet went on to found James Nisbet & Partners, later Nisbets, and recently taken over by Cyril Sweett & Partners.

6   Nisbet, quoted in *Towards a Social Architecture: The Role of School Building in Post-War England*, Andrew Saint, Yale University Press, 1987, p. 119.

7   Geoff Trickey, was a partner, 1967 to 1993 and senior partner, 1988 to 1993. He worked in the National Building Agency from 1965 to 1967.

8   RAE (Dick) Milborne became a London partner in 1964, retired in 1985 and died in 2008.

9   At the time, the so-called Single European Market, commencing on 1 January 1992, was seen as a major opportunity for UK construction firms, not least because of recessionary times in the UK. In the event, there was (and is) much less cross-border activity than expected.

10 The Everest was dropped in 2004 when the firm became Davis Langdon and a Limited Liability Partnership.

Chapter Ten

One Firm One Future

Rob Smith became senior partner of Davis Langdon & Everest in May 2003, aged 54. Like his predecessors, he had been a partner for over 20 years and, like them, he was committed to maintaining the firm that he had inherited. He had become a partner in Davis Belfield Everest when there were eight London partners and he had great affection for the traditional partnership and partnership values. Unlike previous senior partners he did not get a cover of *Building* magazine but he did get an interview and a quirky *Building* photograph with the article.

Paul Morrell, the outgoing senior partner, unlike his predecessors, stepped down but stayed on as a partner. He was younger than they had been (they had all retired at 58) and he was looking forward to getting back into project work. He was also, in any case, heavily involved in the recently established Commission for Architecture and the Built Environment (CABE), Stuart Lipton, the developer, was Chairman of CABE and Morrell was a Commissioner.[1] Although less extrovert than Morrell, Smith was determined to make a difference to the firm during his tenure, he was not content to 'coast' for his period as senior partner.

Since the construction industry came out of recession in the mid-1990s there had been steady growth in demand with a minor drop around the millennium. Davis Langdon had been particularly successful in the five years from 1998 to 2003, led by Morrell. Through natural growth and a series of mergers in the midst of Morrell's term, the firm expanded both nationally and internationally and increased the range of services that it offered. The diagram opposite plots the firm's revenues, profits and qualified staff numbers, all expressed as indices with 1989 equal to 100; 1989 was the first full year after the Langdon & Every and Davis Belfield & Everest merger.

The graph illustrates the slow recovery after the 1990s recession and the rapid growth, particularly in turnover and profits since 2003. It also illustrates turnover and, particularly, profit growing at faster rates than staff numbers. It is now evident that the years from 2003 have been building up to another collapse in construction demand.

In 2008, the worldwide "Credit Crunch" impacted rapidly and extensively on the construction sector into the UK and particulary in London. The first casualties were housebuilders but very quickly Davis Langdon's commercial clients stopped those developments they could. The healthy demand for construction that had been a major contributor to the growth and success of the firm over the past 15 years was over.

Rob Smith, senior partner, 2003–date.
Copyright: John Balsom. Courtesy *Building*.

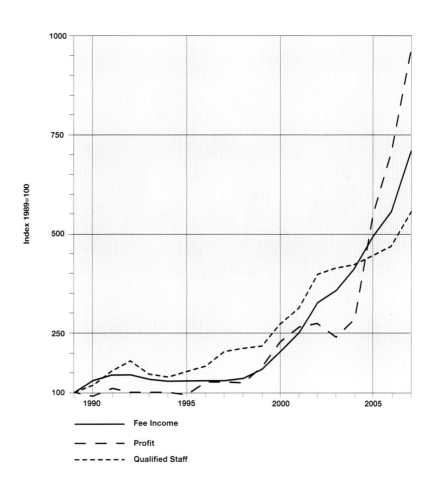

Index 1989=100

—————— Fee Income

— — — Profit

- - - - - Qualified Staff

A New Office

The first major step for the firm in 2003 was to move office from Princes House in Kingsway to MidCity Place, a new office building on High Holborn. The decision on this was made during Smith's previous role as London managing partner. It was the end of their lease although the landlord would have been happy to renew it; they had outgrown Princes House, there were satellite offices in Africa House, Kingsway (MGW), Exchange Court in Covent Garden (Crosher & James and Legal Services) and Theobalds Road (the Finance Department); and there was a desire for more modern space, although less enthusiasm from some partners when it was explained that modern meant open plan. MidCity Place was a newly completed Stanhope building and offered 40,000 square feet on a single floor plate. It is difficult to say whether the move to Princes House in 1990

Graph showing Davis Langdon fee income, profit and qualified staff, 1989 to 2007.

or the move from Princes House to MidCity Place was more of a step change, probably both were in their time. Both put Davis Langdon at the forefront of their competitors in terms of public image and working environment.

The decision was made that everyone in MidCity Place, including the partners, would sit in open plan office space with a range of options for both informal and formal meetings. Adjacent to each block of work stations were small tables with chairs for informal discussion with colleagues; there were quiet rooms, seating three or four, for more focused get-togethers or interviews or for confidential meetings or phone calls; there was a large cafeteria-type area next to reception with both upright and easy chairs and tables that would seat, say, 50 people; and there was a suite of bookable meeting rooms that could accommodate from ten to 50 people in various layouts and combinations.

The move took place over a weekend and was managed with military precision. Staff arrived on Monday morning to find their project and personal possessions in crates by their work stations. Every work station had a desktop computer and a telephone and printing was done centrally on combined copier/printers in 'pods' located strategically around the space. Storage was limited so there was great pressure on surveyors, as natural hoarders, to minimise filing and shelving space.

External and internal views of MidCity Place.

Once everyone had got over the move and adjusted to the new environment, there was almost universal delight in the space and the amenities. The greatest shock was, of course, for partners who were used to cellular offices but even they adjusted quickly to a new way of working. For a long time the greatest complaint was of being shown off to visiting clients and others as they were escorted round the office by proud partners.

A Limited Liability Partnership

In 2004, Davis Langdon, like a number of other professional firms adopted Limited Liability Partnership (LLP) status. At the same time, the opportunity was taken to drop 'Everest' from the name and the firm became Davis Langdon LLP. There were a number of reasons for the changes. It provided reduced personal responsibility for business debts, the LLP itself is responsible for any debts, not the individual partners. Being an LLP also provided the opportunity of spreading the ownership of the firm. Until then, ownership had been restricted to equity partners. Salaried partners received bonuses but had no shareholdings. LLPs allow for a number of types of partners or members. 'C' members are equivalent to the previous equity partners, owner managers; 'A' members are broadly equivalent to salaried partners but now have an equity share in the firm; and 'R' members are equivalent to retired partners during their consultancy period.

Summary of Five Year Trading Results

Consolidated Summarised Profit & Loss Account Year ended 30 April	2008 £'000	2007 £'000	2006 £'000	2005 £'000	2004 £'000
Turnover	196,910	153,974	121,900	106,082	89,812
Operating costs	(148,308)	(113,091)	(90,142)	(81,331)	(78,224)
Operating profit	48,602	40,883	31,758	24,751	11,588
Net financing (costs)/income	25	89	450	(214)	(401)
Profit on ordinary activities before taxation	48,627	40,972	32,208	24,537	11,187
	Average number	Average number	Average number	Average number	Average number
Members and Staff					
Members	225	204	177	151	63
Staff	1,910	1,479	1,229	1,159	1,138
	2,135	1,683	1,406	1,310	1,201

LLP status brought with it the obligation to publish financial results and the opportunity was taken to produce annual reports that projected an image of the firm. Successive reports included items from guest contributors, interviews and dialogues with key clients and presentations of significant projects. They all presented a firm committed to developing its people and their skills along with the obligatory financial data of an annual report.

A New Structure

In 2003, the firm had more than 60 equity partners nationally and the business had a UK turnover of £86 million. There had been structural

Cover of the first *Annual Review*, 2004 to 2005, and table showing trading results.

changes: all partners were partners of the whole firm and the London office share in branch offices had been removed. But the income of partners was still substantially tied to the performance of their office; there was little incentive to refer or share work and every reason to hold on to work and compete with other offices to secure it.

When a partnership reaches a size of more than, say, 20 it becomes necessary to subdivide it into business units. Historically, business units in Davis Langdon were geographically based with individual partners' fortunes largely tied to the performance of their own office. Prior to the 1988 merger of DB&E and L&E, regional (i.e. non-London) DB&E partners only had an interest in their own office; generally, regional L&E partners had no equity share in the business at all, although they did receive a profit share. Since the merger, a variety of equity and profit sharing mechanisms were adopted, all directed more or less at reconciling the two aims of rewarding local performance and fostering national and corporate unity.

A major step forward was to form geographical regions that both encouraged local co-operation and tended to smooth out temporary fluctuations in local financial performance; it also facilitated job and staff sharing and helped to create critical mass. Regionalisation was progressively introduced from the early 1990s and the whole of the UK was organised into regions by the early 2000s. The success of regionalisation emphasised the potential benefits of a single national practice.

Davis Langdon had established and developed its core services, Cost and Project Management, and specialist services, Legal Support, Management Consulting and the others, over the two decades. And each of these had its own champions and leaders who had chosen to focus their career on that service. The number and proportion of non-quantity surveyors and non-members of the RICS had grown annually. But a service based division of the firm tended to create silos of expertise.

Sector specialisms emerged in the 1990s as a response to the increasing complexity of particular building types and the increasingly sophisticated demands of some clients. Morrell and Smith were both keen advocates of this approach. A number of sectors were identified and some were active and successful, in terms of both getting and doing work; while others were less successful. The problem is that some sectors were clear cut but many were not. The challenge is to select the theme or themes that makes groups of projects 'special', building type alone may not do it.

Offices, sports facilities and health buildings, for example, fit the criteria for distinct building sectors. But other groups of projects are not necessarily like that: the defining characteristic may be that they are 'major projects' (projects over, say, £50 million in value); or tall buildings (buildings of more than, say, 40 storeys); or publicly funded projects; or heritage projects, work on listed buildings; or PFI/PPP projects. That is, the key thing may be the type of project or the procurement method or the type of client rather than the building type.

The move to LLP status broadened ownership but did not directly resolve other issues, like profit sharing, that would both incentivise and encourage collaborative working. Traditionally, the focus had been geographical and that will always be influential, if only for practical reasons, but the arguments for ever more offices are less compelling; it is more important that every office has critical mass and capability. Although the number of offices had increased slightly over the last 20 years, generally offices were much larger than they had been. The firm, then had its offices, its core and specialist services and the sectors it worked in. The challenge was how to structure the firm to best service its clients and incentivise its people.

In 2003, Smith put to the partners a revised profit sharing system that attempted to link business plans to business unit and personal performance and a partner appraisal process that took account of both financial and non-financial contributions. The proposal failed to get through a partnership vote, not because it wasn't what many partners wanted but because they didn't think it would work in practice.

The following year, another proposal was put forward with a profit split of 55 per cent local, 27.5 per cent national and 17.5 per cent reserve, the reserve to be allocated at the Management Board's discretion where local action or performance merited it. Share progression was based on a lockstep system but one that permitted downward as well as upward progress, but no more than one step at a time. The appraisal system was also simplified to be less complicated and time consuming than previously. This proposal was accepted although Smith and others saw it as a stop-gap until a better system was devised.

In 2007, the Management Board brought in Margaret Exley of Stonecourt Consulting with a view to helping the firm "become a single company with a unified approach to winning and delivering work." The consultants interviewed partners, organised group sessions and observed practice meetings. An important conclusion was that the geographical division of the firm was no longer helpful. Clients and the firms they worked with were national or, indeed, international and partners were expected to work where they could contribute most. Smith accepted the consultants' analysis and the conclusion that what was needed was a single firm delivering cost and project management with other services collected together in a specialist services' group.

With the experience of 20 years of tinkering with the structure and organisation of the firm, through the merger negotiations in the late 1980s, the debates in the new partnership in the early 1990s and the more recent adjustments to the profit sharing system, Smith felt that something radical was needed. Three working groups were set up on what were seen as the three key issues: Leadership, Organisation and Structure, and Performance Management and Reward. Interestingly, it was the group on Organisation and Structure that was most contentious, possibly because a traditional partnership organisation was clearly inappropriate for a firm with over 200 partners and Performance Management and Reward was only about coming up with a workable system.

The Leadership group decided that the senior partner had too much responsibility and, unsurprisingly, that the management board was too concerned with detail and not enough with strategy. There was a long tradition of at least the appearance of collective decision making. The suggested solution was a separate Executive and a Board with the latter setting strategy and the former delivering it. A five person Board designated by the senior partner consisted of the managing partner, the chief executive, two business group leaders and a non-executive director, a first for Davis Langdon in the UK although the Australian practice had had one for some time. The Board then appoints the executive, including the managing partner, the chief executive, the sector heads and the head of specialist services and a head of service quality and development.

The Performance Management and Reward group initially focused on the first part of their brief. They eventually settled on a set of performance factors including, financial contribution, client management, people leadership, strategic contribution and alignment with the firm's core values. Assessment was to be based on '360 degree' and client feedback. The difficulty, of course, was, and is, deciding how and when the non-financial targets have been achieved. The profit sharing mechanism started from the idea of a single national profit pool with 12 equal profit steps across the business. And the fairness of the system was to be overseen by a Moderation Committee.

The Organisation and Structure group could not devise an alternative system to the traditional geographical structure of the firm that was acceptable to Smith and the Management Board. The group tended to favour a service line based approach and Smith and the board preferred a sector based approach.

The default position was to stick with geography but, instead, Smith at a partners' conference in Gleneagles in Scotland in October 2007 asked the partnership to delay a vote and asked the group to try again to devise an acceptable new structure.

The title "One Firm One Future" was coined for the initiative but it is not a new one. The strapline "One Firm, One Aim, One Future" was used for the merger of DB&E and L&E in 1988. The idea is straightforward enough: to be a single partnership with a single purpose, not a loose network of offices with broadly similar aims and activities, but, as ever, the devil is in the detail.

A new Organisation and Structure group was formed with some changes of personnel from the previous group, with a clear terms of reference and with support from the management consultants. In January 2008 the head of the group proposed a sector focused business unit structure that was accepted by the Board. Over the next three months Smith and the group head met and talked to every 'C' member, the equity partners, and in March 2008 a special resolution was passed.

The new leadership structure was put in place immediately. The photograph below shows the newly constituted Board in January 2009. The appointment of the non-executive director was then pending.

Davis & Langdon Board, on the fourth floor of MidCity Place, 2009. From left to right: Richard Baldwin, Simon Johnson, Rob Smith, Jeremy Horner and Kevin Sims.

The performance management and award system will be introduced gradually. The new performance criteria will be in place for partner evaluations in 2009 but partner remuneration will not be affected until 2010. It, of course, remains to be seen what shape the firm is in in 2009 or 2010; as suggested above, timing is everything.

Sectors

The sectors endorsed by the Board are predominantly based on building type although some are quite specific, for example, commercial, while others are broader, for example, public. They are also, of course, based on recent and predicted patterns of construction investment. The table below sets out the sectors and sub-sectors adopted and their champions. The public sector is the most fragmented and, within that, education, in three sub-sectors. It will be interesting to see how these sectors and sub-sectors evolve over the coming years.

There are offices that act as centres of excellence for each sector or sub-sector and offices that provide support to particular sectors and sub-sectors. Typically, for each sub-sector there are two to five centres of excellence and a similar number of support offices. There is, therefore, good national coverage and all offices are involved in a number of sectors and sub-sectors.

Sectors					
Commercial Paul Allen	**Hotels, Sports, Culture** Peter Flint	**Infrastructure & Industry** Steve Waltho	**Public** John Hicks	**Residential** Mike Ladbrook	**Retail** Richard Taylor
Sub-sectors					
Business Parks	Culture	Aviation	Administration, Defence, Custodial & Justice	Affordable Housing	Development
Data Centres	Hotels & Resorts	Energy & Utilities	Education (Further)	Private Residential	Retailers
Fit-out	Sports & Venues	Industrial, Distribution & Manufacturing	Education (Higher)/Science		
Offices		Pharmaceutical & Process Engineering	Healthcare (Private)		
		Transport & Infrastructure	Healthcare (Private)		
			PFI / PPP		

Commercial

Commercial offices was the first real sector specialism; commercial development and developers had been special interests of Paul Morrell's from the 1980s and he had attracted a group of younger partners, including

Neill Morrison, James Clark, Rob Knight, Paul Allen and Nick Leggett. Since the 1980s, commercial offices have been a major element of Davis Langdon's workload, particularly in London. At the end of 2008 the firm had appointments on a number of London towers including Broadgate, Fenchurch Street, Heron, Leadenhall, Pinnacle and the Shard, though some of these may well become casualties of the current market. Outside London the firm has worked on the Colmore Plaza in Birmingham, St Pauls in Liverpool and the Aurora development in Glasgow. A sub-speciality is office fit-out and that may well provide opportunities in the immediate future as businesses try to do more with less people and less space.

Sub-categories of commercial offices included office refurbishment and business parks; one of the earliest and most influential of the latter was the Stockley Park development in West London.

Hotels, Sports, Culture

From the National Theatre in the 1960s and 1970s to Tate Modern in the 1980s and 1990s and work at Ascot racecourse for 50 years from the 1950s and stadiums all round the world, Davis Langdon has a long tradition of work on cultural and sports projects. They have worked, and are working, on arts projects around the world with the best designers on the most prestigious projects. The firm worked on the 2004 Commonwealth Stadium in Manchester, the 2004 Sydney Olympics, the 2008 Beijing Olympics and is currently working on projects for the 2010 Football World Cup in South Africa and, of course, the 2012 Olympics in London.

Skills and knowledge in sports buildings were developed by Alan Willby. He had worked on the Commonwealth Games in Manchester and brought that to Davis Langdon with the merger with Poole Stokes & Wood in 1999 and joined forces with Jon Coxeter-Smith and, later, James Woodrough. The sports team worked on a number of stadia in Europe and, most recently, form the core of the London 2012 Olympics office in Docklands.

Infrastructure and Industry

Infrastructure and industry are at the less glamorous end of construction but often involve very large projects and innovative procurement and management arrangements. The firm is working nationally and internationally on industrial projects and distribution centres. They are also involved in transportation, air,

Opposite top left: Manchester Civil Justice Centre, Denton Corker Marshall. Photographer: James Maddox.
Opposite top right: Chiswick Park, West London, Richard Rogers Partnership.
Opposite centre: Pineham Distribution Centre for Sainsbury's.
Opposite bottom left: UEA School of Nursing and Midwifery, Norwich, RMJM.
Opposite bottom right: Centre for Mathematical Sciences, University of Cambridge, Edward Cullinan Architects.
Top: Paul Allen.
Bottom: Peter Flint.

sea, road and rail, projects. Most recently they have taken on roles in major energy infrastructure projects, including nuclear, a specialism of Langdon & Every from the 1950s, and renewable.

Public

Davis Langdon has a strong background in public projects, including health, education and physical infrastructure. In recent years much of that has been procured using PFI (the Private Finance Initiative) or PPP (Public Private Partnerships). The firm has worked extensively on the hospital building, schools and further education projects and programmes and has a number of long-term arrangements in place involving a range of the firm's services.

John Hicks had extensive experience in private healthcare with Bupa and Nuffield and built on that to develop an expertise on PFI healthcare projects and beyond that into PFI and the public sector more generally. The firm works in a number of roles on private finance projects, including advisers to the user partner or the provider partner. The rise of these kinds of projects was the final nail in the firm's old contractor rule as a high proportion of service providers were headed by contracting organisations.

Residential

Davis Langdon, and particularly Davis Belfield & Everest, were specialists in public sector housing in the 1950s, 1960s and 1970s, when council house building was at its height, and they have continued to work more recently with registered social landlords, housing associations. The firm now works on three types of residential development: with private commercial developers, with affordable housing providers and with housebuilders. They are involved in projects at all scales, including the 2012 Olympic Village and proposed eco-towns.

Retail

Simon Johnson inherited John Lewis as a client when Geoff Trickey retired. The firm had worked with John Lewis and Waitrose for many years and had also worked with C&A and Debenhams on national programmes but would probably not have described themselves as retail development specialists. In the last decade or so, however, retail has emerged as one of the firms major fee earners.

Top: Steve Waltho.

Bottom: John Hicks.

Opposite top left: Mike Ladbrook, at Broad Road, Sale.

Opposite top right: Battersea Reach, London, Broadway Malyan.

Opposite centre: Refurbishment of Peter Jones, London, John McAslan & Partners.

Opposite bottom left: Refurbishment of Fortnum & Mason, Piccadilly, London, Jestico & Whiles.

Opposite bottom right: Richard Taylor, refurbishment of Selfridges.

Over the years Davis Langdon has worked with most of the major UK retail brands, including Sainsbury's, Marks & Spencer and Selfridges. But they have now moved on to working with retail developers completing major shopping developments including White City, for Westfield in London, and Paradise Street in Liverpool.

These sectoral connections between partners and types of work are not exclusive. Partners also retain strong links with clients and designers. The recession will almost certainly lead to realignments of partners and teams and a more flexible approach to job getting and job doing. But a major construction consultancy needs to be able to demonstrate specialist knowledge and experience in order to be appointed for major projects.

Specialisms are reinforced by selected Cost Models published in *Building* magazine, membership of sectoral organisations, for example, the British Council for Offices, and attendance and speaking at industry events. Partners frequently present at conferences on tall buildings, for example, using information and case studies from the firm's work worldwide. Specialist groups collect and collate key information on design variables and costs so that benchmark data is available to the team and their clients. But, as ever, care, however, has to be taken that confidentiality is maintained among clients.

Commentary

This book was researched during 2007 and 2008 and the final text was written in the early part of 2009. In early 2008 there was some evidence of a downturn in the market, for example, designers reported projects cancelled or postponed, but it was not until Autumn that the so called "Credit Crunch" was acknowledged. Almost immediately, the construction and property sectors felt the impact, initially in speculative housebuilding, house prices and housing transactions, but it did not take long for the effects to spread beyond that to other construction and development projects, particularly where projects depended on private finance. The first small number of redundancies in Davis Langdon came in October and then a larger tranche in November and some staff and partners transferred to the Middle East. It is never so obvious as in times like these that professional services is a people business.

There had been signs of overheating in the construction industry for some time, shortages of staff, high tender prices, increasing orders for new work, particularly private commercial work, so a 'bust' was not unexpected, it was just a matter of time. But the 'bust' that came was not just the usual one that followed a sustained 'boom', this was more systemic. It came after the extent of so-called sub-prime lending and securitisation of 'toxic' debt became evident. The US government sponsored mortgage agencies were effectively nationalised, one major bank, Lehman Brothers, was allowed to go bankrupt and a swathe of banks worldwide had required massive injections of capital in one form or another. In the UK the effective nationalisation of the Northern Rock Building Society in early 2008 had been an early warning but it had been largely ignored. Injections of funds into other major UK banks eventually led to majority shareholdings by the British government.

The first Davis Langdon Forecast article in 2009 in *Building* magazine started off with the following statement:

> Building prices throughout the country suffered a dramatic fall in the fourth quarter last year, dropping by an average of 7.5 per cent as contractors saw a gaping hole in workload ahead of them. The outlook is bleak as private sector construction grinds to a halt and two years of falling prices are forecast.

Later in the article, it commented:

> In the UK, construction is expected to see at least two years of decline, due to a drop off in private sector work across all areas, residential, offices, retail, and industrial. The most recent forecasts point to a 12 per cent reduction in construction by the end of 2010 with an overall recovery not expected until well into 2011.

It will be interesting to see in time how accurate that forecast is.

It seems that the phenomena that had brought sustained economic success, privatisation, de-regulation and globalisation, also contained the seeds of their own destruction. Although these policies were not necessarily fundamentally wrong, the ways in which they were implemented had flaws which, particularly in combination, led to out-of-control effects.

Davis Langdon in 2008 is bigger, stronger and more diversified than it has ever been. It has seen dramatic growth in recent years: it was noted recently that it took almost 90 years to reach the first £100 million annual turnover in the UK but only five to get to £200 million. One result of this recent rapid growth is that 64 per cent of the staff is under 40 years of age and 49 per cent has been with the firm for less than three years. This presents major challenges for a firm that has historically looked back to respect the legacy of its founders while looking forward to maintain and develop that legacy. When growth was gradual and the world was relatively stable, this happened naturally; nowadays it needs a bit more effort and intervention.

Between 1988 and 2006 qualified staff in the firm increased almost sixfold from 153 to 859, an average annual growth rate of ten per cent per annum. Over the same period, qualified staff in the top five firms of quantity surveyors grew at a similar rate. Both Davis Langdon's and the other big firms' growth is partly a result of increased demand and diversification of services but it is also a sign of industry consolidation. As suggested in *QS2000* in 1991, the big firms have got bigger and taken market share from their medium sized competitors.

In early 2009 the firm is adjusting to the effects of the "Credit Crunch" and related impacts on the firm's workload. It may be some years before that £200 million turnover is achieved again. As in previous downturns, the workload will decrease, construction prices will decline, commissions will become more competitive and the firm's income will again depend on reduced fees on reduced values of reduced workload.

Timing is important. The 1988 merger was conceived and consummated in boom conditions; it may not have proceeded if it had been delayed for, say, more than a year. The 1990 recession was almost certainly the worst since the Second World War and the early 1990s were as much about survival as anything else. And, later in the decade, healthy market conditions made the flurry of mergers, PSW, MGW, Schumann Smith, NBW Crosher & James and a number of smaller ones, more attractive to all concerned. More recently, the MacKenzie merger in Scotland was also completed in good market conditions. The current recession is likely to be as bad, or even worse, as 1990 and could be longer lasting. It will be interesting to see how the One Firm One Future initiative plays out.

The graph opposite shows construction output between 1955–2003 at constant 2000 prices. This is the entire graph that is shown in parts on pages 38, 57 and 118. It shows clearly the climbs up to 1973, 1979 and 1990 and the collapses afterwards. The only way now for this graph is downwards; the only question is how far and how fast.

Construction in the UK has declined as a proportion of Gross Domestic Product in the post-war period. Construction output represented around ten per cent or more of Gross Domestic Product (national output) in the 1960s but is now closer to seven per cent. The implication is that, in a mature service dominated economy like the UK, it takes less construction as a proportion of GDP to make the economy run.

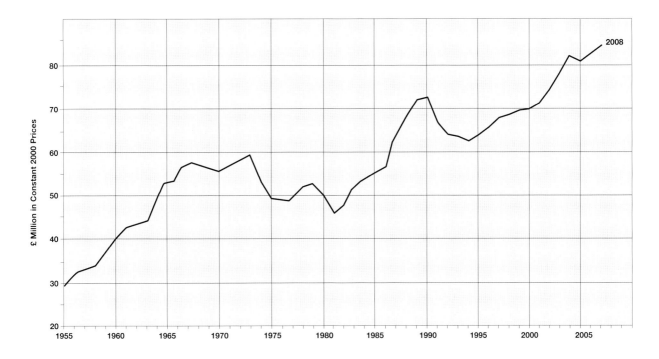

The pattern of construction investment has also changed. Housing for local authorities was a major source of construction demand (around 30 per cent of new output) and workload for quantity surveyors in the 1950s and 1960s but started to decline in importance in the 1970s and is now relatively insignificant (less than five per cent of new output in 2005). By contrast, private commercial new output was less than ten per cent of demand in 1955 but almost a third in 2005. The changes in the pattern of demand are indicative of DB&E's and, to some extent, L&E's early post-war workload and the importance of private sector offices, retail and other commercial work in more recent decades.

Construction and property are cyclical and always have been and Davis Langdon's senior partners have had to cope with their external environment as well as whatever has been happening internally. In the past 20 years there have been two busts and a prolonged boom.

Both busts since 1988 have hit mid-tenure: the 1990 bust in the midst of Geoff Trickey's and Mike McLeod's joint senior partnership (and carrying over into Nick Davis') and the 2008 bust in the midst of Rob Smith's (extended) tenure. That is not to say that Morrell's tenure (1988–2003) was either easy or uneventful. Arguably, some of the changes that Morrell

Graph showing all construction output 1955 to 2008. Source: Office for National Statistics (ONS).

initiated, particularly in terms of regionalisation, specialisation, the quality of office environments and the professionalisation of the business, all set the scene for the changes introduced by Smith. It is obviously essential to adapt and change in difficult times; it is less obvious when times are good.

Since the firm became a Limited Liability Partnership (LLP) in 2004, there is the added complication of corporate transparency. Before the need for annual financial reporting, the partners could keep to themselves the financial performance of the firm so long as they were prepared to take personal 'hits' on their income. Although the firm does not have external shareholders, as an LLP the outside world, and the staff, can see and form opinions on the leadership, profitability and financial strength of the firm. And this can impact on how they are perceived by their clients and collaborators.

With the departure of Rob Smith in the next year or so, the links with the past, for example with the original firms of DB&E and L&E will be weakened and the characteristics of the modern firm, its corporate structure, professional management, financial transparency, etc., will become increasingly significant. The current recession is likely to be at least as deep and as long as its predecessors.

In parallel with the "One Firm One Future" initiative, the firm embarked on a major rebranding exercise in 2008 and the rebrand was launched in early 2009. The new logo appears below, replacing the one launched almost 21 years ago when the merger of Davis Belfield & Everest and Langdon & Every was announced. The rebranding heralded the move to the master brand Davis Langdon for Mott Green & Wall and Crosher & James.

Davis Langdon ⟳☆

Although it is only 90 years since Horace Langdon set up in business in Raymond Buildings, Gray's Inn, the world, the construction industry and quantity surveying have changed more than he could have imagined. Langdon died 50 odd years ago and Tom Every, Owen Davis and Bobbie Everest had all retired by the mid-1970s. Owen Davis lived to see the merger of Langdon & Every and Davis Belfield & Everest and, although he wasn't very happy about it, he was gentleman enough to wish it well. Perhaps he would even have grown to like it. Davis Langdon today would be unrecognisable to the founders both in its size and the range of its services.

But some things remain similar. MidCity Place, the firm's London office is only a few hundred metres from where both Langdon and Davis started in practice, the firm is still a partnership, albeit a Limited Liability one, both their names are in the firm's title and quantity surveying (cost management) is still its main business. Many of the early regional offices in the UK are still there, a number of them have had sixtieth birthday parties. Owen Davis would be pleased to see that the firm still publishes *Spon's Price Books* and that the number of titles has increased; Horace Langdon and Tom Every would be pleased to see that there are still offices in the Far East and the Gulf and that there is still a member of the Seah family in the firm in Singapore.

All of the early partners would be pleased to see that the firm is still working with the best clients and the best designers, and on the best jobs. They would also probably be pleased to see that a number of their old rivals, including Gardiner & Theobald and EC Harris & Partners, are still in business. There would also be some, but probably fewer, contractors' and designers' names still around that they would recognise.

They probably wouldn't recognise, or perhaps even approve of, what the firm does in the name of quantity surveying or cost management but they would appreciate why they do it. Managing cost and procurement was what they did and although they did it with bills of quantities based on a standard method of measurement, they would understand the intent of what is done now. They would be amazed at the computerisation of the firm and shocked at the levels of percentage fees (probably half what they were in their day) but they would recognise that the big expense was still the cost of staff. Finally, with their origins in the 1920s and 1930s, they would perhaps have some words of advice on how to deal with the prevailing economic conditions.

1   CABE took over from the Royal Fine Art Commission (RFAC) as the government's advisor on architecture and the built environment although CABE is much more hands-on than RFAC. Stuart Lipton was a member of RFAC. Morrell was awarded an OBE in the 2008 New Year's Honours list, for his contribution to architecture and the built environment.
2   Consultancies were 'bought out' in 2008. The main reason was the increasing future obligation as the partnership grew.

Explanatory Note on the Firm's Names

The names of professional firms start off as very personal things and, although the significance of individual names may diminish over time, the corporate name begins to take on an importance of its own. Over a period of 90 years or so, Davis Langdon has gone through a number of name changes and changes in style. This has made writing this book difficult in parts: sometimes the firm is referred to as 'the firm' but elsewhere this is not possible. This note, therefore, is intended to outline briefly the principal changes in name and style to the principal elements of the firm. It is not definitive: different conventions were used for official documents, including letterheads, and for written and spoken references and abbreviations; and different terms could be used at the same time, inside the firms and externally.

Horace William Langdon started in practice in 1919 as Horace W Langdon. He was joined in partnership by Cecil Tom Every in 1925 and shortly after the firm became Horace W Langdon & Every. In the 1930s, regional partnerships were formed in the North-West (Langdon Every & Firkin) and in the South of England (Langdon Every & Winship); the former ended in the 1940s when Edward Thornton Firkin left to set up his own practice, the latter ended in 1951 with the death of John Winship. Langdon died in 1954 and, in 1956, the firm throughout the UK became Langdon & Every. It is not clear when 'and' was used and when an ampersand (&) was used; the ampersand seems to have been used in early days on the firm's letterhead but, by the 1980s, it was Langdon and Every.

Two overseas firms were set up in the 1940s: Horace W Langdon & Every (Far East) in Singapore and Horace W Langdon & Every (Arabian Gulf) in Kuwait. The names themselves conjure up the colonial era. On the death of Langdon, the partnership in the Far East, now in a number of locations, became Langdon Every & Seah, including the name of Seah Mong Hee, the senior local partner in the Far East in the title but omitting 'Far East', it was thought to be too restrictive; in the Middle East, the firm's name changed to Langdon & Every (Arabian Gulf).

Owen Austin Davis started in practice in 1931 as OA Davis. He was joined in 1935 by John Belfield and the name changed to Davis and Belfield. Belfield died shortly after this partnership was formed but the name remained. Davis was then joined in 1944 by Robert L Everest and the firm became Davis Belfield and Everest. This was the style used on the letterhead until the mid-1980s. When a new letterhead used a DB&E logo.

Both UK firms were generally known by their initials, L&E and DB&E and, occasionally, DBE. In written form, the 'and' could be written out or an ampersand, depending on the writer's preference. The Far East practice was usually known as LE&S but could be LES.

At the merger of Langdon and Every and Davis Belfield and Everest in 1988, the merged firm's name was Davis Langdon & Everest, with an ampersand, abbreviated as DL&E. In 1994, it was decided to drop the ampersand in the abbreviation and become DLE, although the full name remained the same. In 2004, the firm in the UK became a Limited Liability Partnership, the Everest was dropped and the firm became Davis Langdon LLP. The most common spoken form after the merger was DLE and the change in 1994 was largely to recognise this. Since 2004, DL is a common abbreviation although formally the firm prefers the full Davis Langdon, spoken or written.

The international firm adopted the name Davis Langdon & Seah International in 1990, abbreviated as DLSI and the firm in the Far East became Davis Langdon & Seah, abbreviated as DL&S or, more commonly, DLS.

Generally, in the book, where full names are required, they are given. Where initials are used, typically, they are explained in full the first time they appear in each chapter and, thereafter, they appear as only initials.

There are, of course, many other parts of the firm that have had or have different names and styles. Generally, these are given and explained where they occur. If abbreviations are used, they are explained.

Further Reading

The following publications have been referred to in the preparation of this history.

Adamson, DM and Pollington, T
Change in the Construction Industry,
Routledge: Oxford. 2006

Aston, G
One Hundred Years of Quantity Surveying,
The Annals of Patterson and Kempster, 1860–1960,
Hinds: Dublin. 2007

Bullock, N
Building the Post-War World,
Modern Architecture and Reconstruction in Britain,
Routledge: London. 2002

Chan, CY editor
Post-Merdeka Architecture,
Malaysia 1957–1987.
Pertubuhan Akitek Malaysia: Kuala Lumpur. 1987

Davis Belfield & Everest editors
Spon's Architects' and Builders' Price Book 1975, 100th Edition,
E&FN Spon: London. 1974

Davis Langdon & Everest Consultancy Group
Quantity Surveying 2000, The Future Role of the Quantity Surveyor,
RICS QS Division: London. 1991

Eccles, R & Simpson, K
One Firm One Future at Davis Langdon,
Harvard Business School: Boston MA. 2008

Ferry, DJO
A Study of Quantity Surveying Practice,
RICS: London. 1974

Harris, A edited **Blake, D**
A Chronicle of the Firm of Widnell & Trollope,
Volume One, 1852–1919,
Unpublished. 1974

Hillebrandt, PM
Analysis of the British Construction Industry,
Macmillan Press: London. 1984

Law, NR
History of the Quantity Surveying Profession in South Afric,
Association of South African Quantity Surveyors: Sandton. 1985

Murray, M and **Langford, D** editors
Construction Reports, 1944–1998,
Blackwell Publishing: Oxford. 2003

Nisbet, J
Called to Account, Quantity Surveying, 1936–1986,
Stoke Publications: London. 1989

Nisbet, J
Fair and Reasonable, Building Contracts from 1550, A Synopsis,
Stoke Publications: London. 1993

Nisbet, J
A Proper Price, Quantity Surveying in London, 1650–1940, A Synopsis,
Stoke Publications: London. 1997

Policy Review Committee of the RICS
Surveying in the Eighties, A Strategy for the Surveying Profess
and for the Development in the RICS in the 1980s,
RICS: London. 1980

Powell, CG
The British Building Industry Since 1800,
E&FN Spon: London. 1980

Quantity Surveyors Committee
The Future Role of the Quantity Surveyor,
RICS: London. 1971

Quantity Surveyors Division of the RICS
The Future Role of the Quantity Surveyor,
RICS: London. 1983

Richardson, HW and **Aldcroft, DH**
Building in the British Economy between the Wars,
George Allen & Unwin: London. 1968

Ross Goobey, A
Bricks and Mortals, The Dream of the 80s and the Nightmare of the 90s:
The Inside Story of the Property World,
Century Business: London. 1992

Saint, A
Towards a Social Architecture,
The Role of School Building in Post-War England,
Yale University Press: New Haven and London. 1987

Scott, P
The Property Masters, A History of the British Commercial Property Sector,
E&FN Spon: London. 1996

Skedd, A and **Cook, C**
Post-War Britain, A Political History,
Penguin: London. 1993

Thomson, FML
Chartered Surveyors, The Growth of a Profession,
Routledge and Kegan Paul, London. 1968

Trushell, JM
John Dansken & Purdie, Chartered Quantity Surveyors:
A Case Study of a Professional Practice During a Period of Depression 1919–1939,
unpublished dissertation: University of Stirling. undated

Index

Colophon

© 2009 Black Dog Publishing Limited, London, UK.
 All rights reserved.

Designed by Johanna Bonnevier and Matthew Pull at Black Dog Publishing.
Cover designed by Davis Langdon.

Black Dog Publishing Limited
10A Acton Street
London WC1X 9NG
info@blackdogonline.com

British Library Cataloguing-in-Publication Data. A CIP record for this book is available from the British Library.

ISBN 978 1 906155 71 1

Black Dog Publishing Limited, London, UK, is an environmentally responsible company. *Thinking Big: A history of Davis Langdon* is printed on UPM Finess matt, an FSC certified paper.

architecture art design
fashion history photography
theory and things

www.blackdogonline.com